Fragrant Palm Leaves

Phuong Boi ("Fragrant Palm Leaves") is the name of the monastery founded by several of us in the highlands of central Vietnam, as part of our effort to renew Buddhism. *Phuong* means "fragrant," "rare," or "precious." *Boi* is the kind of palm leaf (talipot palm) on which the teachings of the Buddha were written down in ancient times.

Nhat Hanh

Other Books by Thich Nhat Hanh

Be Still and Know
Being Peace
The Blooming of a Lotus
Breathe! You Are Alive
Call Me by My True Names
Cultivating the Mind of Love
The Diamond That Cuts through Illusion
For a Future To Be Possible
The Heart of the Buddha's Teaching
The Heart of Understanding
Hermitage among the Clouds
Interbeing
Living Buddha, Living Christ
The Long Road Turns to Joy
Love in Action
The Miracle of Mindfulness
Old Path White Clouds
Our Appointment with Life
Peace Is Every Step
Plum Village Chanting and Recitation Book
Present Moment Wonderful Moment
Stepping into Freedom
The Stone Boy
The Sun My Heart
Sutra on the Eight Realizations of the Great Beings
A Taste of Earth
Teachings on Love
Thundering Silence
Touching Peace
Transformation and Healing
Zen Keys

Fragrant Palm Leaves

Journals 1962–1966

THICH NHAT HANH

Translated from the Vietnamese
by Mobi Warren

Parallax Press
Berkeley, California

Parallax Press
P.O. Box 7355
Berkeley, California 94707

Cover and text design by Legacy Media, Inc.
Author photo (1964), courtesy of Eglise Bouddhique Unifiée.

The background images on the cover of this book are the
fragrant leaves of the talipot palm. These long, tough leaves,
native to Sri Lanka and southern India, were made into the
paper on which the Buddhist sutras were first recorded. Just
before the leaves unfurled and separated, they were blanched,
dried, polished, and trimmed into rectangles. The sutras were
then written on both sides of the leaves and bound together.

LIBARY OF CONGRESS CATALOGING-IN-PUBLICATION DATA

Nhât Hanh, Thích.
    [Neo vê cua y. English]
    Fragrant palm leaves : journals, 1962–1966 / Thich Nhat
Hanh.
        p. cm.
    ISBN 0-938077-67-8
    1. Nhât Hanh, Thích — Diaries. 2. Priests, Buddhist —
Vietnam — Diaries. 3. United States — Decription and travel.
4. Nhât Hanh, Thích — Journeys — United States. I.Title.
    BQ974.H37A3 1998
    895.9'22803 — dc21   98-37883
    [B]   CIP

1 2 3 4 5 6 7 8 9 10 / 02 01 00 99 98

CONTENTS

U. S. Journals

1962 — 1963

page *3*

Vietnam Journals

1964 — 1966

page *135*

United States
1962 — 1963

I am in a cabin called "Pomona" in the woods of northern New Jersey. It was so dark the night I arrived that I
was startled my first morning by the beauty and peace-
fulness here. Mornings here remind me of Phuong Boi,
the monastery we built in the highlands of central Vietnam. Phuong Boi was a place for us to heal our wounds
and look deeply at what happened to us and to our
situation. Bird songs there filled the forest, while sunlight collected in great pools.

When I arrived in New York City earlier this year, I
couldn't sleep at all. There is so much noise there, even
at three in the morning. A friend gave me earplugs, but I
found them too uncomfortable. After a few days, I began
to sleep a little. It's a matter of familiarity. I know some
people who can't sleep without a clock ticking loudly.
When Cuong, the novelist, came to spend the night at
Phuong Boi, he was so used to the sounds of Saigon
traffic that the deep silence of Dai Lao Forest kept him
awake.

I awoke to that same deep silence here in Pomona.
Bird songs aren't "noise." They only deepen the sense of
silence. I put on my monk's robe, walked outside, and I

knew I was in paradise. Pomona is on the shore of a lake that is larger than Lake Ho Xuan Huong, in Dalat. Its clear water sparkles in the morning light, and the tree-lined shore reveals leaves of every shape and color, announcing the waning of summer into autumn. I came here to escape the city's heat and to live in the forest for a few weeks before beginning the fall semester at Columbia.

That first morning, the faint sound of laughter teased my ears. I followed the sound even while I was buttoning my robe, and after a short while the path from my cabin opened onto a wide clearing dotted with cabins. There, I saw dozens of children brushing their teeth and washing their faces at an outdoor lavatory. It was Cherokee Village, an overnight camp for seven-to-ten-year-olds, one of the "villages" that make up Camp Ockanickon. That whole first day I played with the boys at Cherokee Village. They had found a golden-colored fawn with white spots named Datino, and were feeding her oatmeal mixed with fresh milk and tender cabbage leaves.

I only brought a few books with me, and I haven't had time to read any of them. How can I read when the forest is so calm, the lake so blue, the bird songs so clear? Some mornings I stay in the woods all day, strolling leisurely beneath the trees and lying down on the carpet of soft moss, my arms folded, my eyes looking up to the sky. In those moments, I'm a different person; it would probably be accurate to say that I am "my true self." My perceptions, feelings, and thoughts aren't the same as when I am in New York. Everything here appears brighter, I daresay miraculous! Yesterday I paddled a canoe more than a mile to the north end of the lake. I tarried among the water lilies and only turned back as dusk began to stain the sky violet. Then it grew dark quickly. If I had delayed a moment longer, I would not have found my way back to Pomona's landing.

The forest here doesn't have *sim* fruit like Phuong Boi, but it does have berries that are just as purple and sweet, called blueberries. Today I went with two eight-year-old boys to pick some, and we stuffed our mouths until they turned blue! The boys talked the whole time. One said he saw a bogeyman last night, a horned devil who thrust his hand into the tent and grabbed the sleeping boys. He said it with conviction, but it must have been one of the camp counselors checking in on them at night. I half-smiled and continued to pick blueberries when the boy stepped back and asked me loudly, "You don't believe me, do you?"

"I do, but only a little," I answered.

"Why?"

"Because what you say is hard to believe. It requires great effort to believe even a little."

He looked crushed. That evening the two boys came

to Pomona and both claimed that they'd seen the bogeyman. They spoke convincingly, and I was forced to
concede.

"Okay, I believe you both."

Satisfied, they returned to Cherokee Village.

On days like this, I long for Phuong Boi. Dai Lao
Forest is much more dense and wild. We even encountered tigers! I dream about Phuong Boi many nights, but
in these dreams, an obstacle always prevents me from
entering. The more I long for Phuong Boi, the sadder I
feel. Phuong Boi was our homeland. As Brother Nguyen
Hung used to say, "Phuong Boi doesn't belong to us. We
belong to Phuong Boi." Our roots are there, deep in the
earth. People say that only sad memories stay with you,
but it isn't true. Those were the happiest days of our
lives, and now, because of our memories, each of us,
wherever we are, turns toward Phuong Boi like a sun-
flower toward the sun.

When we first arrived at Phuong Boi, Nguyen Hung
still lived in Dalat. Our group had suffered so many
disappointments in our efforts to engage the ideals of
Buddhism in the lives of the people of Vietnam. Hung
was ten years younger than I but had already experienced as many disappointments. We all suffered because
of the situation of our country and because of the state of
Buddhism. We tried to create a grassroots Buddhism
that would draw on the aspirations of the people, but we
weren't successful. I wrote articles, published books, and

edited magazines, including the journal of the Buddhist General Association, to promote the idea of a humanistic, unified Buddhism, but within two years the journal's publication was suspended. The Association said it was due to the lack of funds, but it was really because the Buddhist leaders didn't approve of my articles. At one meeting, they declared, "No one has ever used our magazine to preach to us about unifying the Buddhist community!"

We felt lost. Our opportunity to influence the direction of Buddhism had slipped away. The hierarchy was so conservative. What chance did we — young people without position or a center of our own — have to realize our dreams? I became so sick I almost died, so I left the city to live in a small temple in Blao district. Our other friends also scattered to the winds. It felt like the end.

But I couldn't find peace in Blao either. The temple there was also part of the Buddhist hierarchy. From time to time, Sister Dieu Am came from Djiring to visit, bringing medicine and a few oranges. Thanks to her, we were able to muster the courage to make Phuong Boi a reality. Now she lies peacefully in the heart of the earth.

I've been thinking a lot about Phuong Boi's beginnings. In Autumn 1957, I confided to Sister Dieu Am, "We've lost our last anchor. Perhaps our practice isn't strong enough. We need a hermitage where we can devote ourselves to practice. Can you help us?"

She said that she would happily give us Plum Forest

and return to Thien Minh Temple in Hue, but that she
didn't have the authority. How dear and precious her
heart was. I smiled and said, "To ask you to return to
Hue would be worse than us not having a place!" Sister
Dieu Am dwelled at Djiring in the tranquility of Plum
Forest. That is why we named the bridge at the entrance
to Phuong Boi, "Plum Bridge." How beautiful that
bridge was, although it now lies broken and decayed.

The many setbacks had taken their toll on our faith.
We knew we needed a place to heal our wounds, nourish
ourselves, and prepare for new initiatives. Conversations
like that one gave birth to our resolve to build a hermitage, and we chose Dai Lao Forest, a remote and quiet
place with plenty of space, mountains to contemplate,
clear streams, gardens, and paths for walking, as the
place to do it. The thought of such a hermitage appealed
to us like cool water to a desert traveler, like a gift to a
young child. We envisioned a place where we could
cultivate the practices that were needed for the people of
our time. Dai Lao Forest is about four miles north of
Blao, where the highest mountains rise up. At that time,
the forest belonged to the Montagnards, the hill tribes-
people, and was being sold by them quite cheaply. Plots
along both sides of the highway were being cleared for
cultivation or preserved as virgin forest.

The first time we drove up the dirt road into the deep
and mysterious Dai Lao Forest, Sister Dieu Am, Dieu,
and I knew that we were seeing the future. The name

"Phuong Boi" expressed our ideal to serve the roots of our precious Buddhist culture. Phuong means "fragrant," "rare," or "precious." Boi is the kind of palm leaf on which the teachings of the Buddha were written down in ancient times.

This part of the forest was under the jurisdiction of a village named B'su Danglu. After several weeks, Sister Dieu Am, Dieu, and I managed to map out the sixty-acre parcel we wanted, and we offered 6,500 piasters (approximately $90) for it. We weren't trying to take advantage of the easy-going Montagnards. That was the going price for land there, and in fact we offered them an additional 3,500 piasters ($50). We completed the transaction with two friendly men named K'Briu and K'Broi, neither of whom could read or write. But the regional chief of Blao, named K'Bres, and his district chief, named K'Dinh, could.

On a sunny day in August 1957, Tue and I arrived at the chief's office to sign the papers. I signed it "Nhat Hanh," the first time I'd signed a deed. At the bottom of the contract were the fingerprints of K'Briu, K'Broi, and the deputy prefect of B'su Danglu; the signatures of K'Bres and K'Dinh; and my own signature. Thus, I became a property owner, a fact that the communists would later use to denounce me.

It's been raining for days. The roof of Pomona leaks and the books on my desk are getting soaked. I've moved the desk several times, and this morning I think I've finally found a dry spot.

Last night, twenty boys from Ranger Village came to my cabin to hear a talk on Buddhism. I've been the camp's "guest speaker" for most of this month. I've addressed eight groups in all, including the youngest boys from Cherokee Village. The Rangers are the oldest. Each boy brought an armful of wood for the fireplace. On chilly evenings, a warm fire makes Pomona cozy. The boys and I gathered around the fire. I wore the gray trousers and shirt of a novice monk, and I began by telling them that these were the everyday wear of Vietnamese Buddhist novices. "A fully ordained monk should wear a brown robe like the one hanging there in the corner," I told them, "but I like wearing the clothes of a novice. It makes me feel young." Then I put on my robe and explained to them that monks in Vietnam wear brown in order to identify with the peasants, who also wear brown. After that, I put on my *sanghati* robe and told them that this yellow robe is worn only for special ceremonies. I explained about Southern (Theravada) and Northern (Mahayana) Buddhism and spoke a little about Buddhist insight and the similarities between Buddhism and Christianity. Young people are avid listeners and always have lots of questions. Their curiosity is boundless! They asked, "Why do Buddhist temples have curved roofs?", "Are you a vegetarian?", "Can Buddhist monks marry?", "What does Buddhism think about Jesus?" To conclude our session — it was already eleven o'clock — I chanted *Uprooting Boundless Suffering*.

After they left, I put a little more wood on the fire and sat, gazing at the flames, while it continued to pour outside. I imagined it also raining in Saigon, Hue, and Phuong Boi. Brother Thanh Tue wrote that it has been raining in Phuong Boi for weeks and that a section of the Montagnard House roof was blown off by the winds. I don't know if he plans to repair it or let the winds blow the whole house down. We worked so hard to build Montagnard House at the top of the highest hill. The steep slope of the roof made it look like two hands joined in prayer. We spent so many happy hours there — studying, planning, drinking tea, and listening to music — usually sitting on our heels Japanese-style. But when our feet and legs grew tired, we shifted to Cambodian-style, with our legs tucked to one side. We used the lotus position only for sitting meditation. Tonight I envision myself sitting in Phuong Boi with

Nguyen Hung, Tue, Thanh Tu, and Tam Hue, and I smile quietly. Each of us belongs to Phuong Boi, as Hung said. I wonder if Hung longs for Phuong Boi as much as I do?

After buying sixty acres of land, we had no money left, not even enough for medicine (I was still not well). So Uncle Dai Ha and I decided to clear ten acres to plant tea. We hired three dozen Montagnards to help us clear the land, and a month later, when the felled trees had dried, we burned them. Then we had to wait until the beginning of the rainy season to plant the tea. It would be awhile before the tea plants were productive, and we had to find other ways to produce income as well. Brother Thanh Tue went to Saigon to collect royalties that were owed to me from various publishing houses. Sister Dieu Am donated some funds, and that allowed us to continue.

On a sunny morning five months later, Sister Dieu Am, Thanh Tue, and I followed Uncle Dai Ha into the forest and found it transformed into a hill of young tea plants. Uncle Dai Ha had hired Montagnard workers to do the planting. He was such a dedicated supporter of the Dharma. The forest was damp and the trail not well-marked. We had to stop several times to remove leeches from our legs. Uncle Dai Ha wasn't bothered by them at all. Once, he said, his legs were so covered with leeches that he had to rub a bamboo string up and down them to pry the leeches loose. Thanh Tue and I

were only slightly unnerved by them. We stopped and
pulled the leeches off, a little disgusted. But Sister Dieu
Am screamed every time one attached itself to her leg,
and we had to come and rescue her. After a few months,
even she managed to overcome her fear.

In the summertime, we could wander at ease. But the
leeches returned as soon as the forest became damp
again. Uncle Dai Ha explained, "They don't die in the
summer, they simply dry up. When the rains come, they
revive." He told us of a time when one of his workers
picked up what seemed to be a twig to use as a toothbrush, when suddenly the "toothbrush" began to squirm.
It was a leech revived by the man's saliva. He threw it to
the ground and had to go get some water to rinse his
mouth several times. Mountain people rub a kind of
ointment on their legs to repel leeches, or they carry
limestone, the kind chewed with areca nut. If you rub a
little limestone on a leech, it will fall off.

We walked along sharing stories, and in no time
reached the hill of tea. Montagnard Hill was the highest
in the forest. Looking from that spot, the sky was perfectly blue and the clouds pure white. Distant mountains
swathed in clouds looked like islands rising from a sea.
On a clear day, we could see the vast landscape stretched
out below. Every morning for two years, I walked up
Montagnard Hill, and each time I found Phuong Boi
more beautiful than before. Some mornings the fog was
so dense, you could barely see your hand in front of your

face, but even then, it was a joy to stand on Montagnard
Hill. One morning when the forest echoed with bird
songs, Hung and I walked up Montagnard Hill from the
meditation hall. When we reached the peak, we saw two
deer dancing among the tea plants. In the morning light,
their coats looked like golden silk dappled with white
stars. We stood perfectly still, not wanting to frighten
them, and we watched them play on the hill of tea.
Then, bounding, one after the other, they disappeared
into the south forest. We were speechless.

Although the hill was planted with tea, it still looked
wild and uncultivated. We walked between the rows of
tea plants, over and around the many tree stumps that
remained. Uncle Dai Ha told us they would rot away
within a few years, so there was no need to uproot them.
The earth there was soft and fragrant. We circled the
hill, then paused at the edge of the forest where Uncle
Dai Ha intended to clear fifteen more acres for buildings
and a garden. A year later, when Nguyen Hung moved
in with us, the tea plants were already producing a small
yield, and Sister Dieu Am proposed that we clear another five acres and plant more tea.

At the same time, we began constructing a two-story
community house at the foot of Montagnard Hill. The
upstairs would serve as a meditation hall, and the
ground floor would be a library, a study, a dormitory, a
kitchen, and a living room.

I managed to sell another manuscript, *New Discoveries*

about Buddhism, but we still faced financial difficulties. We asked everyone we knew for help. Besides Sister Dieu Am, those who helped the most were Nhu Thong, Nhu Khoa, and Uncle Dai Ha's family.

While the buildings were going up, the workers met with much hardship just getting in and out of Phuong Boi. One truck, even with tire chains, could not climb the muddy hill to deliver the wood and supplies we needed. Uncle Dai Ha had to burn another road four hundred meters long through the forest. I was the geomancer, determining which way to orient the buildings to assure well-being. Perhaps my lack of skill in *feng shui* is why we no longer have Phuong Boi and are all scattered to the winds. I should not have accepted the assignment.

Sister Dieu Am traveled from Plum Forest every week to join us, and her health prospered from the hard work and hiking. Even Nhu Khoa, a robust young man, couldn't keep up with her! We wanted to move into Phuong Boi in time for the rainy-retreat season, so we doubled our efforts. By then the road was cleared, and we could enter Phuong Boi by crossing a bridge and following the path to the foot of Montagnard Hill.

If only I could spend the rest of my life walking in that beautiful forest! The trail was fragrant with *chieu* blossoms and many other flowers. Just reaching Plum Bridge, at the entrance to Phuong Boi, lifted my spirits. I felt I had *arrived.* And the rest of the path was even more pleasant. Then, unexpectedly, Phuong Boi and Montagnard Hill appeared around the bend. Zen Master Thây Thanh Tu loved to stroll there wearing his wide straw hat and leaning on his staff.

The wind and rains arrived just before the start of the retreat season, and transporting things in was difficult. We had beds, bookcases, a small stove, and many other things to get ready. Tue was teaching in Bao Loc and was unable to help much. Hung and I spent long days putting the finishing touches on the meditation hall, trying to create a feeling of simplicity and harmony. In this meditation hall, we didn't sit on the floor but on platforms. The Buddha on the altar was painted by my elder brother, Thây Giai Thich, and its expression was one of serenity and joy.

One afternoon, as Hung and I stood on the balcony looking down at Meditation Forest, we saw a cloud stretching like an unfurled bolt of silk from the forest's edge to the foot of Montagnard Hill. We ran down the hill to stand next to the cloud, but it disappeared. So we climbed back up the hill, and there it was again! Filled with pines and other majestic trees, Meditation Forest was the most beautiful part of the forest. Our plan was to make narrow walking paths and also a few places where one could sit in meditation or quiet reflection. There were many varieties of flowers for us to pick for the Buddha's altar, but our favorites were the *chieu* and *trang* blossoms.

Nhu Ngoc and Nhu Thong promised they would
come from Saigon for the Opening Ceremony. As luck
would have it, it poured that day. Nhu Khoa had lent
Hung and Tue a jeep to transport two thousand books
for our library, but over and over, the jeep got halfway
up the hill and slid back down. It took the whole day to
get the books up the hill and unload them. On Hung's
last trip, carrying a handsome bookcase donated by
Nhu Thong, it began to rain so hard that Hung and
Thanh Tue looked like muskrats! I was shelving books
when I saw them, soaked to the bone and shivering. I
wrapped Hung's feet in blankets and began to light a
fire for Tue to dry himself, but he insisted on driving
back to town.

Mrs. Tam Hue served us dinner at seven o'clock, the
first meal at our new kitchen table. Hung was so cold he
refused to join us. Finally he agreed to sit at the table,
and I offered him a bowl of rice, urging him to take at
least one bite. Reluctantly, he picked up his chopsticks,
and soon he was happily eating and conversing, allow-
ing Mrs. Tam Hue to fill his bowl three more times!
That night he slept soundly, with no sign of even a cold.
The next morning, Tue returned to Phuong Boi and
told us that after he'd returned to Bao Loc Temple, he
changed into dry clothes, poured himself a cup of hot
tea, and drifted off to sleep while waiting for his tea to
cool. Oblivious to the world, he slept the whole night.

Hung and I stayed overnight at Phuong Boi for the

first time. The doors were not yet hung, and strong winds blew down a wooden beam, waking us with a crash! We listened to the howling wind and knew a typhoon was not far away. There we were, in the middle of the forest, far from civilization. Our only desire was to put down roots, to build a home in the forest and create a safe territory. After the crash, we couldn't get back to sleep, so Hung and I lit a fire and talked until the first bird songs and the howling gibbons announced the coming of dawn. Then we climbed up Montagnard Hill and saw the east blushing with the pink of dawn. Fog concealed the distant mountains.

Phuong Boi was a reality! She offered us her untamed hills as an enormous soft cradle, blanketed with wildflowers and forest grasses. Here, for the first time, we were sheltered from the harshness of worldly affairs.

Next Wednesday I'll leave here and return to New York. Autumn has arrived. Here they call it "fall," because so many leaves fall from the trees. They call the first season "spring," when young buds spring forth from the branches. Riverside Park must be beautiful now. Princeton is always beautiful in the fall. At Princeton, I always walked down a narrow path bordered by emerald green grass. It is so cool and crisp this time of year. At the slightest breeze, leaves fall from the trees and brush against your shoulders. Some are golden, some as red as lipstick. There are unimaginable varieties of hues. Leaf showers are a joy for the eyes. At home, I love the trees that change their colors, like the *arjun*. Dai Lao Forest is always green. Very few trees in Dai Lao Forest lose their leaves.

Princeton is beautiful, but it doesn't have the beauty of Phuong Boi. Fog never encircles the mountains, making you feel as though you are standing at the edge of the sea. The scent of *chieu* flowers does not waft through Princeton, nor do gibbons' cries echo there. Princeton is not untamed, like Phuong Boi.

I will never forget the nights when the moon shone

over the forests of Phuong Boi. Nighttime in the forest is not like nighttime in the city or even on a farm. At night, the sacred forest declares its absolute authority. The curtain of darkness is thick and secretive. Sitting in the study at Phuong Boi, I heard many eerie cries coming from the forest. By eight o'clock it was already night, and the forest's dominance was restored. The whole universe sank into a profound silence that, at the same time, vibrated with life. I could almost hear the majestic steps of the mountain god as he leaped between the towering trees.

On full moon nights, none of us could sleep. One time, I was up late writing when Thanh Tue rose from his bed and stood quietly by the window to gaze at the moonlit forest. I blew out my candle with a whisper and stood beside him. When moon and forest were together, they created a profoundly marvelous and mysterious atmosphere, unlike any we had experienced before. The silence was total, yet we could hear moon and forest speaking to each other. They were no longer two, but had become one. If you took away the moon, the forest would cease to be. If you took away the forest, the moon would not be. We wouldn't be standing by the moonlit window if moon and forest ceased to be. We were mesmerized.

Some nights I stood gazing at the forest for hours. Just fifty meters away, the omnipotent forest pulled at me, with an irresistible force. It was wild and invigorating. I imagined seeing the shadowy form of a Montagnard tribesman from thousands of years ago, and I could feel the ancient tribesman in myself awakening. I felt the urge to leave civilization behind, throw away my bookish knowledge, tear off my clothes, and enter the forest naked. To do what? I didn't know. But I would enter the forest's depths. Even if wild animals devoured me, I knew I would feel no pain, terror, or regret. I might even enjoy being devoured. I stood at the window for a long time, struggling with the call of the forest and the moon.

The forest in Medford, by comparison, is tame and meek. I long for Phuong Boi. Sixteen moons have passed since I left Vietnam. The other day I wrote these lines:

On the pillow of forest's deep night
I dream of the sixteenth-day moon.
Sixteen moons have come and gone.

On the nights at Phuong Boi when there was no moon, I'd look up at the night sky and imagine the fullness of the sixteenth-day moon. Sixteen moons and the sixteenth-day moon are one, yet two.

On the first day of the rainy-retreat season, it stopped raining. Nhu Thong, Nhu Ngoc, and Thây Chau Toan arrived at nine in the morning with offerings for Phuong Boi. We filled a beautiful vase with wildflowers to offer to the Buddha. I remember vividly the bowls, plates,

chopsticks, and food. Montagnard Hill was too overgrown for us to eat outdoors, so we ate in Montagnard
House. Tue had arrived. Nguyen Hung and I were
putting the final touches on the meditation hall. Toan
went into Meditation Forest to pick flowers, and he was
soon joined by Sister Dieu Am and Sister Luu Phuong.
The two sisters gathered snow-white *chieu* flowers, and
Toan picked a few peonies and many branches of *sim*
blossoms. We filled many small vases, mostly with ar-
rangements of *sim* branches. Toan had removed the
leaves to make them look like peach blossoms. We filled
the largest vase with *chieu*, peonies, and some flowers we
didn't even know the names of. Toan cut a large pine
branch and set it in a brown-glazed Montagnard vase in
the meditation hall. Nhu Khoa and Thanh Gioi hiked
over the hills into Phuong Boi and joined us. What a
wonderful gathering! After a ceremony honoring the
offerings, we gave everyone a tour of Phuong Boi.

Our friends stayed until mid-afternoon, and we discussed future plans. Toan, Nhu Ngoc, and Nhu Thong
were the first to leave. To return to Saigon, they had to
cross the forest to Dai Ha Village, where they could
catch a bus. Nhu Khoa and Thanh Gioi were the next to
depart. Finally, Uncle Dai Ha's family left, as did Sister
Dieu Am, Sister Luu Phuong, and Thanh Tue. Thanh
Tue couldn't join us permanently. He still had a teaching
job in Blao.

That evening, a tranquil emptiness returned to

Phuong Boi. After bidding farewell to Sister Dieu Am
and Tue, we entered the gateway to Meditation Forest,
marked by a board nailed to a tree on which were
painted the Chinese characters "Dai Lao Mountain,
Phuong Boi Hermitage." Phuong Boi was a reality! It
was not like anything we had known before. It was
precious beyond words. We never thought we would
come into contact with such a reality, yet it seemed like
a cloud that could dissolve at any moment. I agreed
with Hung's sentiment — we did not own Phuong Boi;
Phuong Boi owned us. Later, Ly called Phuong Boi "the
Pure Land." Wherever we traveled, we would always
belong to that Pure Land.

We climbed Montagnard Hill that evening to look
out in the four directions. Then we walked between the
rows of tea bushes — the earth was so spongy — and
along the edge of the forest and down into a dale. It was
there that Hung saw the fresh footprints of a tiger
leading in the direction of Plum Bridge. It was already
dusk, and the forest was deserted. A little anxious, I
suggested we return to Montagnard House. We crossed
through the tea bushes to the top of Montagnard Hill.
When we reached our quarters, we built a fire, as the
night was growing chilly. Aunt Tam Hue was unable to
stay that night, so Hung and I were the only ones there.
Others planned to join us a few days later. We prepared
a simple meal of rice and mustard green pickles with
soy sauce, and then, sitting together by candlelight,

shared our thoughts about what we might accomplish in the coming days. Before going to sleep, Hung and I celebrated a brief ceremony to express our gratitude.

When it was raining, mornings in Phuong Boi were exquisite — vital and bursting with life. On chilly mornings I didn't rise early, especially since I'd usually been up late writing. Hung and Tue knew that my health was still frail, so they were careful not to disturb me when they woke up. Aunt Tam Hue didn't need much sleep at all. By the time I woke up, she had tea steeping and after we practiced sitting meditation, a pot of rice-and-mung-bean porridge ready for us to eat. We sat in front of the warm stove drinking tea and eating breakfast in our cheerful kitchen.

The morning sun was bright, but not hot. So we warmed ourselves through physical labor. After just ten minutes of work, we felt comfortably warm. Hung and I were both handy with a hoe and a spade, but it still took several months to clear Montagnard Hill of brush and brambles. I don't know how many tables we managed to make from the rattan and wood we cleared. We also put up swings and hammocks, where visiting monks from Hue and Saigon would rock gently for hours. No matter how old they were, all the monks loved to swing and sit in hammocks.

Mornings at Phuong Boi were as pristine as a blank sheet of paper, pure white except for a pink blush along the edges. We awoke with the awareness that twenty-four brand new hours were before us, and we would not allow anyone or anything to violate this time of ours — no meetings, appointments, or waiting for buses. The whole day was for us. We would tend the tea bushes, clear the forest underbrush, plant fruit trees, write, study, or do whatever we wanted to do. We all worked hard at many things, yet we never tired, because everything we did, we did by choice. If one person didn't feel like weeding around the tea bushes, someone else usually did. If no one felt like clearing the forest, it would wait for another day. We did whatever we wanted. After breakfast, someone would suggest a morning project. By that time, the residents at Phuong Boi included Hung, Tue, Trieu Quang, Ly, Nam, Phu, Aunt Tam Hue, and myself. If Nguyen Hung suggested, "Let's clear underbrush on Montagnard Hill," two or three others would likely be interested in joining him. Or if Ly suggested, "Let's spend the morning making a path that winds down to the valley," there would always be someone willing to work with him. Consensus was easy to reach. If there was more than one proposal, we divided into teams, according to individual preferences. From time to time, instead of working, we went for a hike together. After preparing a picnic lunch, we walked through the forest, stopping along the way to rest by a stream. Hung and Trieu often returned home with exquisite orchids. At the end of a hiking day, we all slept soundly.

At Phuong Boi, there was no dress code. We could

wear whatever kind of hat or boots we liked and tie any
manner of belt around our waist. Sometimes, glancing
in the mirror, I noticed that I looked like a hobo. Sometimes I didn't shave for a week, not out of laziness, but
because there were other things I enjoyed doing more!
When we went on our hikes, we wore garments of
thick, rough cloth to protect ourselves from thorns. We
tucked our pant legs into our rubber boots to discourage leeches. We slung sacks over our shoulders to carry
our lunches, a hammock, or a first-aid kit, and each of
us held a walking stick. If any of my students had seen
me in my hobo garb, they would have been shocked.
This was not the proper dress for a classroom discussion on classical poetry.

Living in the mountain forest, our strides and ges-
tures grew bold and strong. Instead of joining palms
and bowing to greet each other in the traditional manner, we raised one hand up high and waved. We didn't
walk along the mountain paths with measured, stately
steps. We walked fast, and often we even ran. We yelled
to one another from one hill to the next. Nguyen Hung
could yell louder than anyone, and his voice was as
shrill as a train whistle. In fact, everyone who spent
time at Phuong Boi loved to shout. Once Hung climbed
a tall pine tree in Meditation Forest to cut a branch,
and he let go a whoop so loud the whole forest rever-
berated. I was straightening the meditation hall, and his
shout startled me so that I dropped my broom and ran

outside to look. What is even funnier is that I shouted right back. The forest was so immense, we felt minuscule. I think we shouted to overcome our feeling of being utterly insignificant. It was also our way of compensating for the many social conventions forced upon us in the past. In the conventional world, we had to speak with restraint, guarding each word. Society dictates how we must eat, greet each other, walk, sit, and dress. When we came to Phuong Boi, we wanted to cast off all of these rules and conventions. We ran and yelled to shatter social restraints and prove to ourselves that we were free. Here in America, people greet each other by asking, "How are you?" Everyone agrees that the way it is asked is meaningless, but if you don't ask, others feel as though something is missing. It's especially odd when you visit a doctor. He asks, "How are you?" and you answer, "Fine, thank you." If you were fine, why would you be visiting the doctor?

What makes nature's voice so compelling? The call of moon and forest was irresistible. The storms of the monsoon season also called to me. Even as a young boy, I've always been enchanted by storms. Thunder rumbled, the black sky sank low, and the first raindrops, large and heavy, spattered on the roof tiles in our village. Gusts of wind banged against the window shutters. When I saw and heard those signs, I was transported to another realm. They were the prelude to a majestic symphony. After a crash of thunder that seemed loud enough to

crumble the earth, the rain began to tumble like a water-
fall. How could I sit still at such a moment? I ran to the
window, threw back the curtains, and pressed my face
against the glass. Areca palms bowed as earth and sky
moaned and screeched. The universe shuddered. Large
leaves whipped ferociously against the window. Rain
pounded down and gushed in the gutters. Birds strug-
gled against the wind that shook silver curtains of rain.
In the symphony of the storm, I heard a call from the
heart of the cosmos. I wanted to turn into an areca tree
or become a branch bending in the wind. I wanted to be
a bird testing the strength of its wings against the wind.
I wanted to run outside in the rain and scream, dance,
whirl around, laugh, and cry. But I didn't dare. I feared
my mother's scolding. So instead I sang for all I was
worth. No matter how loud I sang, my voice could not
be heard above the roar and crash of the storm. As I
sang, my eyes stayed glued to the drama taking place
outside the window. My spirit was absorbed by the
storm's majesty. I became one with the storm's powerful
music, and I felt wonderful! I sang one song after another. When at last the storm subsided — it always
seemed so abrupt — I stopped singing. The excitement
in my body quieted, but I could feel a few tears still
clinging to my eyelashes.

I still respond to the call of the cosmos, although the
way I do so has changed. The call is as clear and compelling as it was those many years ago. When I hear it now,

I pause, and, with all my body, with every atom of my being, every vein, gland, and nerve, I listen with awe and passion. Imagine someone whose mother has been dead for ten years. Suddenly one day he hears her voice calling to him. That is how I feel when I hear the call of sky and earth.

Just yesterday, I knelt by the window to listen to a symphony of rain, earth, forest, and wind. The window was open, and I didn't close it. I just knelt there, my head bowed in respect, and I let the rain drench my head, neck, and robe. I felt so at ease, so complete. Only when I began to shiver from the cold did I stand up and close the window. I changed out of my wet robe and lit a fire, while the forest of Medford billowed in the ecstasy of the raging storm.

18 *August 1962*
Medford, New Jersey

Conversations between moon and forest and dramatic thunderstorms are not the only times I hear the call of the cosmos. I also hear it during the stillness of midday. At midday in the Vietnamese countryside, a rooster's melancholy crow is the only sound for miles. The sun-blinded streets are deserted. North, south, and central Vietnam all share midday stillness. I do not agree that evening is the saddest time of day. To me, evenings are always beautiful and happy. Evening, like morning, is active, full of change and vitality. It is not a time of fading. Evening announces the arrival of the full array of night life, when nature is so active. Humans rest at night, but moon, stars, water, clouds, insects, and grasses throb with life. The time I would call sorrowful is midday, around one or two in the afternoon.

At midday, all natural activity comes to a halt. There isn't a voice to be heard. There isn't even a thread of wind, and the trees are as still as corpses. The dormant sky stretches beyond measure, and the sun hypnotizes the earth and her myriad creatures with its fierce and fiery eye. Then, at the nudging of a cloud, the earth begins to turn once more, and the spell is broken. If you've ever awakened from a nap at the exact moment that the sun paralyzes the earth, you will hear the call. I have heard it hundreds of times, and each time my heart trembles. Barely awake, the sea of my subconscious mind floods my being. I hear the universe calling me home, and my whole body responds.

I heard that call four times at Phuong Boi. Never had trees stood so still or sky stretched so high. My being was overcome with an intense longing to return, to follow that ineffable call. I felt as though I were standing at a threshold obscured by dense fog. If only I could dispel the fog, I would be able to see. See what? I did not know. But I was certain it would reveal my deepest longing.

I remember the first Tết — Vietnamese New Year — we celebrated at Phuong Boi. Four days before Tết, three friends — Trieu Quang, Tu Man, and Thanh Hien — arrived, like children returning home for the holidays. Quang brought armfuls of plum branches covered with spring buds. We all pledged to celebrate the biggest Tết of our lives. After a night of discussing details, we agreed to build a huge bonfire, simmer a large kettle of earthcakes to make the traditional offering before midnight, set off fireworks at midnight, eat our earthcakes, and welcome in the New Year, all on Montagnard Hill.

None of us will ever forget that bonfire. In order to plant tea, we had felled more than one hundred trees, burned them, and then dragged the charred trunks into great piles for firewood. For two days, we chopped those trunks into logs, some three meters long, and our completed woodpile was as big as a house. In the heart of the pile were plenty of dried grasses, leaves, and kindling. Our bonfire burned all night long, and there were still red-hot coals on the second day of the New Year. We'd pitched tents in order to camp near the bonfire. A few friends did not want to spend the whole night on Montagnard Hill, fearing the chilly morning mist. But after considering it further, they realized that the bonfire itself would chase away the mist and cold. In fact, at times it was too hot!

Ly, from North Vietnam, claimed he could wrap earthcakes as well as anyone in the north. At first we thought he was exaggerating, as writers are wont to do, but after seeing him at work, we knew it was true. Aunt Tam Hue bought the sweet rice and mung beans and gave Ly just the right long, green *đong (phrynium capitatum)* leaves to wrap the cakes. I always enjoy wrapping cakes, so I served as Ly's assistant. I helped him wash, cut, and fold the leaves. He made a small mold from wood to shape the earthcakes perfectly square. They needed to be simmering in water by five-thirty in order to be ready before midnight. Man and Hien built two campfires near the foot of Montagnard Hill, one for the kettle of earthcakes and another to boil water to add to the cake kettle as needed.

Everyone contributed to our Tết preparations. This

spirit of cooperation made it a real Tết. Nguyen Hung
and Trieu Quang spent the afternoon chopping down
bamboo, which they sawed at the joints, stacking the
pieces alongside our tents.

While the earthcakes were simmering, we showered,
and then gathered around the main tent to relax. We
listened to Saigon's end-of-the-year broadcast on our
Sony radio, shared a simple meal, and then each of us
shared what was going on in our lives. At that time, the
only full-time residents of Phuong Boi were Hung, Ly,
Tue, Aunt Tam Hue, and me. Our other friends were
like birds, coming home from the four directions. We
chatted happily about all the events and changes in our
lives since we'd last seen each other. We all knew that
Phuong Boi was our true home, our *alma mater*.

On the branches of tall trees left standing on Montagnard Hill and all along the banister of Montagnard
House, Man and Ly hung lanterns. At ten-thirty, Hung
gave the orders to light the bonfire, and in a few minutes
it was ablaze. Flames leaped so high that we were worried we might start a forest fire. Fortunately, the forest
was more than 400 meters away. Because Montagnard
Hill was the highest point, the fire cast a circle of light
over the whole forest. The animals must have been
surprised. We could make out Uncle Dai Ha's house on
a distant hill, revealed in the flickering play of light and
shadow. By eleven o'clock, the flames were licking the
sky. We returned to the meditation hall to make our

New Year's offerings. The simple ceremony lasted just twenty minutes. At midnight, Hung, Man, Quang, Hien, and Ly began to toss the bamboo pieces onto the fire, and they exploded with a loud crackling noise. The bamboo served as our "fireworks." More than fifty pieces of bamboo were thrown into the fire, and not one failed to pop. We must have frightened every animal in the forest.

Ly's earthcakes were delicious. Several factors contributed — Ly's talent for preparing earthcakes, the special atmosphere of Phuong Boi, the deep understanding and happiness we shared, and, perhaps most of all, our hunger. Following tradition, Aunt Tam Hue, the eldest among us, shyly offered each of us a simple, deeply felt greeting, and then each of us offered good wishes to every other person, totaling fifty-four New Year's greetings in all!

On New Year's Day, we divided into three small groups to explore the forest, stopping along the way to build small fires and toss more bamboo firecrackers onto them. Thây Thanh Tu wasn't there for our first Têt, but the following year he had as much fun as we did taking part in these kinds of boyish games.

It was easy to feel like a family at Phuong Boi. Even Thây Thanh Tu changed his way of greeting to a more boisterous one. He began to hike, arrange flowers, and garden in the free, open style of Phuong Boi. From the first time he came to visit, Thây Thanh Tu felt a deep

connection with Phuong Boi. He asked us to reserve a
small space on Montagnard Hill for him to build a
hermitage. I told him he should consider Phuong Boi
his home. In just a few months, with help from some of
his friends, we did build a hermitage for him on the
slope of Montagnard Hill, and we called it "Joy of
Meditation Hut." In a chant offering food to the Buddha, the phrase "the joy of meditation as daily food"
describes the spiritual nourishment gained by meditation. Thây Thanh Tu was pleased when we suggested
this name. Near Joy of Meditation Hut, we dug another water tank. Thây Thanh Tu built a beautiful
trellis in front of his hut for flowers, and he planted
more flowers all around. Along both sides of the path
leading down the hill, he planted pine saplings from
Djiring.

By the time Joy of Meditation Hut was completed,
construction had already begun on Montagnard House.
Trieu Quang and Nguyen Hung did most of the work,
with the help of two Montagnard friends and Mr.
Phuong, who lived in the village. Because Montagnard
House would be exposed to wind and other elements
on the hill's summit, great effort was made to build it
solidly. Yet in only two short months, the graceful
structure was completed. I helped decorate both the
interior and exterior. Montagnard House soon came to
symbolize all that Phuong Boi meant to us. We prac-

ticed tea meditation there most afternoons and sitting meditation in the evenings. We often slept there as well. But on cold, windy days, we had to gather up our bed-rolls and take refuge in the more protected house at the foot of the hill.

I'll never forget the magical nights standing on the balcony of Montagnard House, gazing at the moon and stars, which seemed close enough to touch. From that balcony, the evening star was as big as the moon! Many nights, I dragged Ly away from his manuscripts to look at the night sky. I, too, liked to write at night, but on those kinds of starry nights, writing was impossible.

I hear that Phuong Boi is no longer safe and that Thây Thanh Tu had to abandon Joy of Meditation Hut to return to Phu Lam. When I left, I thought he would be able to stay there in peace, but it seems I was wrong. Yesterday, in a peaceful, loving state of mind, I wrote him this letter:

Dear Thây,

I have found the Truth. Hearing such a boastful statement, you are probably breaking up in laughter. But I mean it. When I encountered Truth, I was startled. It was nothing out of the ordinary. It was someone I'd met long ago, someone I've known intimately for a long time. Why has it taken me so long to recognize it, more than ten thousand lives?

When I saw it, I was so surprised, all I could do was burst out laughing, just as you must be doing as you read this.

I said, "I thought with a fancy name like Truth, you'd be more beautiful."

"You think I'm ugly?" Truth asked.

I looked again and had to admit that Truth was not ugly.

Truth then asked, "Now that you've seen me, what will you do tonight?"

I answered solemnly, "When I'm hungry, I'll eat. When I'm tired, I'll sleep."

Thây, on the day I departed from Tan Son Nhat Airport, I brought with me an egg. I still have that egg with me. I've been incubating it for several years, like a chicken sitting on her own eggs. Friends who went with me to the airport didn't know about it. The customs officials didn't notice it either, so I said nothing. But sitting in Joy of Meditation Hut, Thây, I believe you knew. I told you about it once and promised you that I would let you know when it hatched. Do you remember? With another year of incubation and favorable conditions, the chick has cracked its shell and stepped into the light. Its rapid growth rivals that of the child-warrior Phu Dong.

On May 7th, I witnessed a conversation be- tween the Buddha and Mara. Buddha received

Mara on Vulture Peak as an honored guest. It was wonderful. I will write down their conversation and offer it as a sutra:

Buddha: Please have a seat.

Mara: Thank you, Sir. That assistant of yours, Ananda, is so difficult. When I announced my arrival, he refused to let me see you. He said, "What business have you here? The Buddha defeated you years ago at the foot of the Bodhi Tree, and he certainly will not receive you now. You are his enemy." But he was forced to let me in when I countered his arguments.

Buddha: (laughing) What did you tell him?

Mara: I asked, "So the Buddha has enemies now?" A Buddha with enemies is not a true Buddha. Your attendant obviously understood that, and he let me in.

Buddha: You always triumph over others using trickery. You wouldn't be Mara if you didn't.

Mara: Exactly. My dear Buddha, let me tell you what is troubling me. People dress me in paper clothes and paint my face to look cruel and stupid. They say I breathe the dark smoke of suspicion. That's the only form they give me. Wherever I go, I am feared and despised. It's really no fun being Mara.

Buddha: You think being a Buddha is fun? Businesses use me to sell their products. Devotees carry

me on floats and drag me through streets filled
with boutiques on both sides, selling coal, fish
sauce, and who knows what else? Don't think
you'd be happier as a Buddha.

Hearing this, Mara burst out laughing.

I wrote this letter to Thây Thanh Tu in a peaceful,
loving spirit. In the future, if we are ever able to return
to Phuong Boi, I'll place a copy of it on the table in
Montagnard House.

It's been quite cold the past few days. Day after tomorrow I leave for Princeton for a few days and then I'll return to New York. I feel restored by my stay at Pomona. I've hiked, canoed, and swum. I've done all the things the children do — nature walks, crafts, ping-pong, and volleyball. I've run races, helped put on skits, and played games. The children always walked with me back to Pomona when they had time. We've really enjoyed each other's company.

Last night there was a ceremony to celebrate the end of camp. It was a reminder of the Indians, or Native Americans. I was invited as an "honored guest" and given a long green feather. The children performed traditional Native American dances in the dark forest. Then, at nine-thirty, they walked in the dark to the ceremonial site. There were five hundred children, and each of them kept perfectly silent. I was impressed. When they reached the site, the groups sat down in their appointed places. Beneath the starlight, I could see the dim outline of a woodpile. Everyone waited without making a sound.

At exactly ten o'clock, an eerie, ancient-sounding cry

arose from the depths of the forest. Then a drum began beating to announce the arrival of the elders. A moment later, three shadowy figures stood before the woodpile. One made a sign over the pile and recited a prayer asking the sacred fire to return. His voice inspired awe. After a few moments there was a crackling sound followed by a flash of blue sparks, and then the pile burst into flames. As the fire grew brighter, the three figures came into clear view. They were three boys dressed in loincloths, their bodies and faces darkened with stripes of paint, with feathers in their hair.

One of them gave a command for the ceremony to begin. First the dances were performed. I could tell how ardently the children had practiced. Dressed in traditional garb, they did their best to express the spirit of the dance and the tribe they represented. The audience watched in silence. No one even whispered or fidgeted, and no matter how spectacular a performance was, no one applauded. My favorite dance was one in which two youths fought using flaming torches to win the favor of a woman. We all sat riveted, watching the fierce struggle, until at last one youth was victorious.

After the dancing, a ceremony was held to present honorary feathers to those campers who'd shown themselves to be exceptional in the "nation" of Ockanickon. An elder called out the name of a youngster. Echoes followed the call from the four directions and then a short drum beat. The echoes sounded mysterious, as though they issued from spirits who had come to witness the ceremony.

I couldn't help but think of the tribal people in B'su Danglu, and our Montagnard friends who often passed through Phuong Boi to gather *ria* greens. The tender inner leaves, tinged with violet, are edible. Because *ria* leaves grow in pairs, Ly dubbed them "twin-leaf." The Montagnards sold many things they harvested from the forest to city-dwellers — bamboo, rattan, orchids, and venison — but they never sold *ria* greens. They told us that these greens prevented leg cramps. I think they also contain an element that relieves arthritis, and Uncle Dai Ha said that they were also a cure for insomnia. From time to time we'd pick some precious *ria* greens and ask Aunt Tam Hue to make soup from them. Our Montagnard friends did not prepare soup from the greens. They crushed the leaves, added a little salt, and then steamed them. It was their favorite dish. One afternoon, Miss Phuong, the botany professor, came from Saigon. She gathered some greens that she thought were *ria* greens and made soup. After consuming the *"ria"* soup, we all felt a little high. We had a lot of fun teasing our good-natured friend about that — the botanist who couldn't recognize the right greens!

Sometimes when a party of Montagnards passed through Phuong Boi, we'd invite them in for tea. Most of them could speak a little Vietnamese. Among us, only Uncle Dai Ha spoke Montagnard, and he never had time to teach us. I did find a mimeographed copy of a Vietnamese-Montagnard dictionary. I remember exactly where we kept it in our library.

We all felt a special kinship with the Montagnards. We found them to be honest and sincere. Unfortunately, many Vietnamese tried to cheat them, and today most Montagnards are less open and direct.

The Montagnards are uncommonly robust, far more resistant to disease than most Vietnamese. They pay little attention to sanitation, yet they seldom fall ill. But when a Montagnard does get sick, it is often serious, even fatal. Once I encountered a Montagnard family passing through Phuong Boi. One man was carrying his father on his back. The old man was old and gaunt, his limbs thin as reeds. The family told me he was dying of old age and not illness, and so there was no cure. They knew his death was imminent and were carrying him to the place he wished to die.

Another time, I saw a Montagnard mother bathing her toddler in ice-cold spring water. The weather out-side was also cold, and it made me shiver just to watch them. Yet the child endured the cold without a whimper. A city child given a bath like that would probably catch pneumonia. Aunt Tam Hue said that the Montagnards bathe even their newborns in cold water. They are dunked in a cold stream several times. Those able to withstand it grow strong and healthy. Those who can-not, die. I don't know if that's true, but it might explain why the Montagnard population remains constant, neither increasing nor decreasing.

I'll never forget the afternoon we were planting white plum saplings with Uncle Dai Ha and a group of Montagnard hunters passed by. They carried bows and poison-tipped arrows. We stopped working to speak with them. Uncle Dai Ha translated for us. It was the first time I ever held a poison arrow. Uncle Dai Ha explained to us how they made the yellow poison.

To witness their skill as archers, Ly asked one of them to shoot an arrow. He indicated a curved branch at the forest's edge as a target. The man fitted a non-poisoned arrow into his bow and drew it. The odd twang of the bowstring and the whoosh of the arrow made me think his arrow had gone astray. But no, with a sharp thud it hit its mark exactly. We cheered before the arrow even stopped quivering.

We were impressed by this band of hunters who were obviously still in touch with the old ways of their people. Such a band of hunters, we thought, could travel anywhere in the jungle without fear. This romantic sentiment prompted Trieu Quang to ask them what they did when they saw a tiger in the forest. Their answer was brief and to the point: "We run." We burst into laughter, and the hunters looked at us with a puzzled expression. They'd answered honestly and simply. They couldn't imagine the fierce battles with tigers we'd been imagining!

Uncle Dai Ha, who understood the ways of the
Montagnards and the forest far better than the rest of
us, explained, "The tigers in this region do not kill or
eat humans. They eat deer and other animals, which are
plentiful here, unlike in some of the partially cleared
forests near Quang Binh and Quang Tri. Tigers only
attack humans when they are forced to live in too small
a territory. If you encounter a tiger in this forest, it
won't attack if you stay out of its way. That's what the
Montagnards mean."

Tue laughed until tears came to his eyes. It was a
good thing we'd met up with a good-natured party of
Montagnards. In the city, such laughter could have
engendered hard feelings or even a fight. But it was
hard not to laugh. The hunters' answer was in such
contrast to our naive ideas.

One day, Aunt Tam Hue's son, Phuong, was bicy-
cling up the path to Phuong Boi. Just ten meters into
Meditation Forest, where the path swerves to the right,
he encountered a huge tiger lying in the middle of the
path. Its back was turned to Phuong, and it seemed to
be gazing at the distant mountains. Phuong froze in
fright. Most of us caught in the same situation would
probably faint. Mr. Tiger gave no sign that he was
aware of Phuong's presence, though Phuong was no
more than three meters away. Phuong was afraid that if
he turned around and rode away, the tiger would hear
the sound of his bicycle and attack him from behind.

Advance or retreat, neither option was attractive. So
Phuong came up with another plan. He decided to
frighten the tiger into running back into the forest. He
picked up his bike and smashed it to the ground as he
gave a blood-curdling scream. It didn't even startle Mr.
Tiger. He simply stood up slowly and ambled back into
the forest, without even glancing back.

I was checking our eucalyptus cuttings when I heard
Phuong's scream. I ran at once in the direction of the
scream and found Phuong, as pale as a skinned chicken,
lying on the ground next to his crumpled bike. I called to
Aunt Tam Hue and together we helped Phuong to the
house. It took him more than three days to regain his
senses, he'd sustained such a fright! It was fortunate that
the tigers of B'su Danglu do not eat human flesh, or we
would have been in danger more than once.

In ancient times, some Vietnamese chose to live in the
highlands among wild beasts. They preferred the danger
of being eaten alive to living under an oppressive regime.
Of course, Phuong Boi was not filled with threatening
beasts. It was a beautiful, peaceful, and magical place.
But what was it that had driven us to abandon city and
village life? The Buddhist hierarchy did not accept us,
especially Ly and myself, because we were determined to
speak the truth. Now I understand that truth and virtue
must be joined by strength. When I first read the French
author La Fontaine many years ago, I was disturbed by
this statement: "The argument of the strongest party is

always the best." *(La raison du plus fort est toujours la meilleure!)* Since then, decades have passed, and life has taught me more than once that his statement is at least partly true. Truth without strength cannot stand firm. Strength does not have to mean tyranny or violence, but one must be strong. Without strength, how could those with no more than a pen challenge powerful authorities?

Every one of us — Man, Hien, Huong, Tue, Hung, myself, and many others — was unable to find a place in the Buddhist hierarchy. We were accused of sowing seeds of dissent when we challenged anything traditional. We were considered rabble-rousers who only wanted to tear things down. The hierarchy did not know how to deal with us, so they silenced our voices. For eight years, we tried to speak about the need for a humanistic Buddhism and a unified Buddhist church in Vietnam that could respond to the needs of the people. We sowed those seeds against steep odds, and while waiting for them to take root, we endured false accusations, hatred, deception, and intolerance. Still we refused to give up hope.

Now some of those seeds have begun to grow. As discontent with the political regime is growing, the idea of a Buddhism for the people is taking shape. We couldn't imagine then how deeply our ideas would take root, especially in central Vietnam. One afternoon while accompanying Nhu Hue and Nhu Van on a visit to a poor hamlet in Quang Nam, I heard a mother singing one of Tam Kien's protest songs to lullaby her child to sleep! I wanted to weep.

Of course, one cannot expect too much too soon. Casting off the old skin is not something a culture does overnight or without resistance. The fear of challenge is often accompanied by a subservient mentality. And if there is subservience, culture is not true culture, just a tool for controlling others. Hardships and conflicts caused by challenges to the old cannot be avoided. That is why the path of struggle is the only path worth following.

We continued our activism even after we moved to Phuong Boi. Though we spent many days exploring the forest, reciting poetry, and just enjoying ourselves, we also devoted hours and hours to studying, discussing, and writing about a new, "engaged" Buddhism. Ly almost always stayed up past midnight working on manuscripts. My health didn't permit me to stay up that late, but I worked as hard as I could. In addition to research and writing, I began to compile a Buddhist dictionary. Before I left Vietnam, I handed the unfinished manuscript to young friends at the Buddhist Institute in Nha Trang and asked them to complete it.

It makes me happy to remember our study sessions in the library. Nguyen Hung and Thanh Tue were especially diligent students. I occasionally introduced lesser-known sutras, and these sparked wonderful discussions. Ly was always the most eloquent. In fact, sometimes we had to subdue him. Thây Thanh Tu said very little, simply smiling gently. Sometimes we asked him to lead the discussions, and I remember one wonderful discussion on Zen that he led when a group of Buddhist students from Saigon came for a visit.

Trieu Quang didn't speak much either, but when he did, his words would usually spark a heated debate. Most of all, Quang loved to work in the forest. He cleared a beautiful area at the forest's edge, which he called "Paradise Lawn." He wanted to raise a calf there, but we opposed the idea. Tue laughed and said, "At least we'd have fresh milk in the mornings!" I was afraid the calf would attract tigers.

One day Quang met a band of Montagnards passing by carrying a small, bound deer. Quang purchased the deer in order to raise it in Paradise Lawn. No one opposed him, but the deer, despite being untied and treated with loving care, refused to eat anything we offered. Finally on the fourth day, Quang thought to offer the young deer some milk, and it lapped it up enthusiastically. After that, it began to prance about Paradise Lawn, and the next morning, it was gone. It went back into the forest, like Datino, the quick-growing fawn adopted by the Cherokee campers. Every child wanted to take him home, but I suggested they release Datino back into the woods. Some of the children looked disappointed, but finally they agreed.

The summer of Quang's deer, many sad events befell

us. Sister Dieu Am became ill and had to be taken to Dr. Sohier's clinic. Ly was arrested. I had to flee to Saigon, and everyone else was forced to move to a nearby strategic hamlet set up by government troops for "protection." It all began with visits from government security agents, who suspected us of clandestine activities. Although they didn't identify themselves, we knew they were agents by the way they questioned us. We lost our sense of security, and watched the demise of our paradise, piece by piece.

I recall every detail of that summer's events. Only three days after Nhu Hien told us that Sister Dieu Am's condition was improving, we received a telegram that she had taken a turn for the worse. Hung and I hiked down to the road to try to get a ride to the Sohier Clinic in Dalat to see her. We waited from ten in the morning until four in the afternoon without luck. Every bus was filled, and every car ignored us. Finally, at just past four o'clock, our friend Nghia passed by and agreed to take us to Dalat. Though he drove as fast as he could, the road seemed to drag on forever. When we finally reached the clinic, Sister Dieu Am had regained consciousness and was out of danger. She smiled weakly, her bright eyes revealing her joy at seeing us.

After a period in Dalat, we moved Sister Dieu Am to Saigon for further treatment at Grall Hospital. Then she returned to Hue, where the climate was more conducive to her recovery. In three months, her strength began to return. Before I left the country, she appeared confident and in good spirits. I sat by her bedside in Thien Minh Temple and spoke with her about the projects we would share in the future. Though she appeared tired, her smile was bright and energetic. I explained I would be gone only nine months, and that when I returned, I was sure the situation would be better and we'd be able to accomplish a lot. I tried watering seeds of faith in her. I was sure she would recover. But our dear sister died only three months later. When I received the news, all I could do was slowly write down these words in my notebook: "I will miss you, Sister. " Then I knelt down to pray for her. I was sure that the hour she passed away, she held all of Phuong Boi and all of us in her thoughts. I also took comfort in knowing that Hung was with her when she died, as were Thanh Hien, Nhu Hien, and Nhu Lien. When I return, Sister Dieu Am will no longer be there. I will stand by her grave in Tu Quang and speak to her from my heart. I know she isn't dead. Someone like her can never really die. She lived a beautiful life, active and rich in faith. All of us carry her image within. We grieve her passing, but we smile tenderly every time we think of her.

I remember visiting Sister Dieu Am at Grall Hospital on Vietnamese New Year's Eve, 1960. It was a sad Têt for Phuong Boi. Nguyen Hung had been forced to return to Hue, and everyone else had scattered to different provinces. Thây Thanh Tu, Thanh Tue, and Aunt

Tam Hue were the only ones who dared stay at Phuong Boi. I wasn't afraid to stay, but everyone insisted I leave for my own safety.

I settled at Bamboo Forest Temple in Saigon, and began to work with a group of college students to organize the first courses for what would become the School of Youth for Social Service. The most dedicated students were Khanh, Duong, Chieu, Phuong, Chi, Nhien, and Cuong, and they all understood the importance of their roles. I was expected to attend the New Year's Eve gathering they'd organized, but instead I went to visit Sister Dieu Am in the hospital. I spoke with her, read her a Têt newspaper, and stayed with her to usher in the New Year. That year people were forbidden to explode firecrackers. I lit some pink candles next to the flowers I'd brought her as a New Year's gift. At one a.m. I wished her a Happy New Year and a restful night's sleep. I walked alone from the hospital back to the temple. There were no cars on the street that late. I passed the Presidential Palace with its garish Christmas lights and smiled sadly at such arrogance.

Five months later, Ly had to be hospitalized at Co Doc Hospital in Phu Nhuan, when the severe headaches that he'd suffered in the past returned. Ly is a man of great strength and courage, but when he's in extreme physical pain, he cries uncontrollably. Shortly before his headaches returned, he and Hung had accompanied Thây Duc Nhuan down to the road to catch

a bus. Afterwards they walked the five miles to Bao Loc
Village. While shopping for a few supplies in the market, Ly was approached by a security agent with a
warrant for his arrest. Hung accompanied them to the
police station, determined not to return to Phuong Boi
without Ly. The police demanded a statement from Ly.
He asked for a pen and sat and wrote until nightfall.
When he ran out of paper, he asked for more. When at
last he was finished, the police escorted Ly and Hung to
Bao Loc Temple to spend the night. The next morning
they returned for Ly to extract yet further statements.

I was working on the *Buddhist Dictionary* when Hung
returned. He told me what had happened and handed
me a piece of paper on which Ly had written, "If I don't
return, please finish my book for me." I was deeply
moved by his words. Our friends urged me to leave
right away for Saigon. It seemed that the authorities had
been watching us for some time, perhaps to retaliate for
the articles and books I'd written opposing their poli-
cies. In that situation, you could be accused of being a
Viet Cong by anyone who opposed you. Who would
believe what we had to say? I prepared to leave for
Saigon, hoping there might be something I could do to
help Ly. I asked Tue to telegram me right away if Ly
was released. I also left instructions for Ly to come to
Saigon if he was released.

The wait for word from Ly seemed endless, but I
finally received a telegram at noon the next day: "Please

let us know whether Sister Dieu Am's illness has improved." I was greatly relieved, because I understood the message. Ly had been released.

Shortly after Ly came back to Saigon, his headaches returned. I took him to the hospital and entrusted his care to Phuong. Fortunately, Ly's condition improved within a month. The day I left Vietnam, Ly seemed anxious. He urged me to go, as did all my friends, saying there was nothing I could do at home given the current situation. Ly gave me a book as a parting gift, which I only opened upon arriving at Princeton. On the last page were two lines in his handwriting:

> *On the day you return, if the sky is torn asunder,*
> *look for me in the depths of your heart.*

Those lines filled me with dread. I knew the situation at home was becoming increasingly tense. Discontent with the regime was growing. Phuong Boi was slipping through our fingers. Ly predicted a violent upheaval and collapse of the government. I trembled and thought only about the day of my return. I prayed for everyone I loved.

A strategic hamlet was set up next to the highway. At first Thây Thanh Tu, Tue, and Aunt Tam Hue stayed on at Phuong Boi, but before long, they, too, were forced to leave. Thây Thanh Tu and Aunt Tam Hue moved temporarily to Dai Ha and occasionally checked on Phuong

Boi. Tue returned to his teaching position and visited Phuong Boi once or twice a week. I mourn for Joy of Meditation Hut. I mourn for Montagnard House. I mourn for every leaf and blade of grass at Phuong Boi.

Before leaving the country, I paid an unannounced visit to Phuong Boi and spent the night there. In the morning, a cold mist shrouded the sky. I bade farewell to Thây Thanh Tu, to Phuong Boi, and to all my books, and I offered these lines as a tribute to Thây Thanh Tu:

> *Clouds softly pillow the mountain peak.*
> *The breeze is fragrant with tea blossoms.*
> *The joy of meditation remains unshakable.*
> *Forest offers floral perfumes.*
> *One morning we awaken,*
> *fog wrapped around the roof.*
> *With fresh laughter, we bid farewell.*
> *The musical clamor of birds*
> *sends us back on the ten thousand paths,*
> *watching a dream as generous as the sea.*
> *A flicker of fire from the familiar stove*
> *warms the evening shadows as they fall.*
> *Impermanent, self-emptied life,*
> *filled with impostors whose sweet speech*
> *hides a wicked heart.*
> *My confidence intact,*
> *I bid farewell with a peaceful heart.*
> *The affairs of this world are merely a dream.*

Don't forget that days and months fly by
as quickly as a young horse.
The stream of birth and death dissolves,
but our fraternité *never disappears.*

Thây Thanh Tu was visibly moved. I told him, "I am leaving now, but I'll come back." I've thought of Thây so many times since then.

One day I read the following couplet in my notebook:

Meeting up we laugh. Ha Ha!
Falling leaves flood the forest.

Suddenly I thought of Phuong Boi and was filled with longing. "Meeting up we laugh. Ha Ha!" That's exactly how it was when we crossed Plum Bridge and climbed up Montagnard Hill to greet each other.

But enough, enough. Phuong Boi has slipped through our fingers. I mourn for each thicket, each glade, each path. Even someone as gentle and unthreatening as Thây Thanh Tu is no longer allowed to sit in meditation in the lap of Phuong Boi. What does the future hold? We've fled in the ten directions. How much has Phuong Boi fallen into ruin? Will Montagnard House remain standing through wind and rain until our return?

We can never really lose Phuong Boi. It is a sacred reality in our hearts. No matter where we are, just hearing the name "Phuong Boi" moves us to tears. Yesterday

I wrote to Man and told him that though hurricanes and gales have flung us in opposite directions, faith will return us to each other.

Medford is cold now. The campers have all returned home, and it grows ever more silent here. I've spent so much time thinking about Phuong Boi, and, the more I do, the more peaceful and full my heart grows. I suspect that all the other "birds" of Phuong Boi think about Phuong Boi as much as I do. The woods of Medford have also offered me many peaceful hours. Perhaps when I return to New York, my images of Phuong Boi will be intertwined with images of Medford.

Almost no one is here. Most students and faculty are home for the holidays. It's snowing outside, and Brown Hall, my old familiar home, is bathed in the stillness of a late December evening.

I arrived the day before yesterday, and I'll be able to spend three weeks of winter break on the beautiful Princeton campus. What a wonderful Christmas gift! I've been so busy in recent weeks, I'm quite happy to leave it all behind for now. Before leaving New York, I visited a few friends at Columbia, including Professors Friess and Cerbu. I stopped by Binh and Bach Lan's restaurant and held Tam Tuyen, their baby daughter. I've been so busy, I haven't had time for such simple pleasures. Then I packed my bags and stopped by my office to check on my mail. I saw Miriam, the department secretary, putting the final touches on the end-of-the-year faculty party.

Miriam said, "The dean would like to invite you to join us."

I answered, "I regret I won't be able to. I'll be leaving for Princeton in a few minutes."

"What a shame! Well here, have a piece of cake now."
Both cake and red wine were set out for the party.

Miriam cut me a piece of cake, which I ate, walking
back and forth to warm up. I was still shivering from the
cold.

She suggested, "Drink a little wine. It will warm you
up."

"Thank you, " I said, "but my face turns bright red
after even a drop."

I telephoned a friend who had offered to take me to
the Port Authority Bus Terminal. The Port Authority
was packed with travelers. I bought my ticket and stood
in line for half an hour before getting on the bus. Thank-
fully, the terminal was heated. As soon as we were all on
the bus, it pulled away.

This was the second time I'd taken the two-hour bus
ride along the New Jersey Turnpike from New York to
Princeton. The rivers, lakes, and streams we passed
were frozen, and fog obscured our visibility. By the time
we reached New Brunswick, it had begun to snow.
Everyone seemed to be absorbed in images of a cozy
Christmas Eve with their families. They had shopping
bags filled with brightly wrapped parcels with red ribbons — Christmas gifts for their loved ones. Outside,
the snow continued to fall silently. The only sound was
the hum of the bus's engine traveling down the highway.
I, too, was touched by the spirit of the season. But my
thoughts turned to sweet rice, New Year's greetings

painted in Chinese characters on red banners alongside doorways, evening markets bursting with ripe watermelons and peach and plum branches, pedicab drivers happy to have so much business, and soldiers along the border listening to gunfire and longing to return home.

When the bus stopped, I stepped out, a small bag in each hand, and walked in the gently falling snow to Brown Hall. The empty campus was beautiful. Snowflakes covered my head, and I felt cold even though I was bundled up in a coat, hat, scarf, and gloves. When I reached Brown Hall, there was no one in sight. I managed to find my Indian friend, Saphir, who gave me the key to my room. I was glad to take off my coat and unpack. I turned up the heater, made the bed, and stood at the window gazing at the falling snow. I was happy to be back at Princeton. My heart felt at rest.

Yesterday, Saphir and I went out shopping in his Volkswagen bug. The college cafeteria and snack bar are closed for the holidays, so we have to eat in restaurants or prepare our meals in the Campus Center kitchen. Saphir and I bought rice, cabbage, milk, and a few other things, and, together, we prepared a simple meal that we ate in the kitchen.

It's brutally cold outside. Though it was not snowing this morning, I didn't dare venture out. The announcer on WPRB advised against it. He said it was three degrees below zero. I spent the whole day in my room. Around noon Saphir brought me a small plate of food and a carton of milk. This evening it is snowing again, and the cold seems to have abated somewhat. Saphir and I plan to walk over to the Campus Center, about a hundred yards away, to prepare a hot meal.

Winter will drag on here until the end of March. Snow is beautiful the day it falls, but three or four days later it hardens and becomes rather dirty. A poor hamlet back home would be transformed after a night of snow. Vietnam doesn't have snow, but it does have beautiful scenes that Princeton doesn't, like coconut trees reflecting in rivers and city streets bursting with bright red flame tree flowers. Winter here lasts so long that just about everyone feels impatient for spring to arrive. After nights of heavy snowfall, plows are needed to clear the roads. Because it is so cold, the snow then turns to ice, and it isn't unusual for someone to break an arm or a leg slipping on an icy path. Icy paths here are far more dangerous than the swampy paths back home. When it snows heavily, I wear rubber boots over my regular shoes to prevent my feet from getting wet, or I'd surely catch cold. I really don't want to get sick over here, as I have no friends or relatives to call on to take care of me. I try my best to guard my health.

Besides the bright whiteness of new snow, winter here offers only one other color: melancholy gray. The green lawns have disappeared. The trees are bare. It is as though the earth's vitality has been squeezed from her. One day near the end of autumn when all the leaves had fallen but the brutal cold of winter had not yet arrived, I looked out at a row of bare trees, and tenderness filled my heart. I understood deeply that, like animals, trees are sentient beings that need to prepare for their future. Not so long ago, the same trees offered cool shade to the rows of houses, but now they stood austere and stripped, ready to endure another long winter. Their bony arms printed stark patterns on the gray sky, the same sky that was hidden, not so long ago, by their foliage.

When icy winter comes, it is unforgiving to all things young, tender, and insecure. One must grow beyond youthful uncertainty to survive. Maturity and determination are necessary. Seeing the courageous, solid way that trees prepare for winter helps me appreciate the lessons I've learned. I thought about Ly's poem, and I shuddered. Our homeland is about to pass through a devastating storm. The oppressive regime, relying on force to satisfy its greed, has caused too many injustices. Discontent is increasing, driving many people to join the National Liberation Front. The regime's injustice, oppression, and corruption feed the opposition every day. The government is responsible for creating this explosive situation. Nine years have passed since the treaty with the French, and an opportunity for something better has been lost. The storm will break at any moment. We can't hide our heads in the sand. We must be like the trees. We must dispel all indifference and uncertainty, and be ready to face the storm. We cannot remain attached to our youthful innocence. We must strengthen ourselves for the coming test.

After my autumn reflections on trees, I had two especially vivid dreams. That night I had a cold. I didn't improve after taking some cold medicine, so I asked Steve to spoon my back with Vick's Vapo-Rub, an American version of Tiger Balm. I showed Steve how to stroke my back vigorously with the edge of a Chinese porcelain spoon until my back turned bright red. It is a common form of massage in Vietnam. Thanks to Steve's spooning, the chill in my back went away, and I felt much better. Steve thought spooning to be a rather strange custom. No one over here would dream of treating an illness by bruising the patient's back. I took another cold pill and covered myself with a blanket. I left the jar of Vick's and a pitcher of water on the night table next to my bed, and fell asleep.

In the first dream, a young man stood in the doorway of a large, empty room, about fifteen or twenty feet from me. I wasn't sure who he was, but I recognized that he was someone very dear to me. I also knew that he was vulnerable and needed my protection. When I think about the dream now, I still can't identify the young man. Hung? Chau? Phuong? Tue? Toan? Perhaps a composite of all my friends. Then a monstrous, hideous brute entered the room, and his enormous hands reached out to snatch the young man. He meant to kill him. The giant was too far away for me to stop him. I felt paralyzed, as though my feet were glued to the floor. Then in my desire to protect the young man, my instincts took over and, with all my might, I threw a heavy object at the monster. But he was quick. He caught it, and I realized with horror that I had thrown a handsaw. Without meaning to, I had supplied the giant with a deadly weapon to use against my brother. The giant laughed, as if to mock my suffering, and then he sawed the young man in two, as easily as cutting a young banana tree. I plunged into an abyss of grief and woke up, my head as heavy as stone.

After awhile, I fell back to sleep and had a second dream. I was standing in a large room that was filled with tables and chairs, and I spotted a tiny, copper turtle, just like the ones that are used to hold candles on altars in the Vietnamese countryside. I didn't know what the turtle was for, but I sensed it was precious and sacred. I could also see that the turtle was deathly ill, and that its death was somehow connected to my own. Worried for the turtle, I found some Tiger Balm and rubbed a little on its back. I began to spoon the turtle's shell, taking great care. But the turtle began to cry and, with horror, I realized my efforts had only made its condition worse. I looked closely and saw a fine crack on the turtle's shell. The Tiger Balm had penetrated the shell and was burning the turtle's tender skin and organs. The turtle was dying. Panic-stricken, I looked for a towel to wipe off the balm, but it was too late. A strange, secret voice in my heart told me the turtle was dead. Feeling desperate, I knelt down to pray. I didn't know who to pray to, but kneeling was the only way I could respond to the hopelessness that was consuming my soul. The turtle's corpse shuddered, as though some hidden force was squeezing it, and then it exploded, shooting streams of water everywhere. One stream was coming straight at me. I jumped out of the way and the water fell to the floor. The water turned into a small button-like object that began to spin like a top. When it stopped spinning, I saw that it was a flower with four white petals.

Then the scene shifted, and I was standing alongside a road strewn with corpses. Men were tossing the bodies onto the backs of large trucks with such force that many of the corpses broke in two, as though they were made of porcelain. The trucks revved their engines and sped off, leaving me alone in a cloud of red dust. At that moment, I woke up, my heart pounding. I felt paralyzed by pain. Finally I managed to lift my hand, and I lightly tapped my forehead. I did my best to smile, but my room seemed shrouded with the horrifying atmosphere of these dreams. My forehead, pillow, and nightshirt were drenched with sweat. With effort, I sat up, wiped off the sweat with a towel, and changed my clothes. I didn't try to go back to sleep. I lit a candle. The lamp would have been too harsh. I massaged my arms and legs to get the blood moving again, and reviewed the dreams in my

PARALLAX PRESS
PO Box 7355
Berkeley CA 94707

Parallax Press publishes books and tapes on mindful awareness and social responsibility — "making peace right in the moment we are alive." It is our hope that doing so will help alleviate suffering and create a more peaceful world.

For our complete catalog of books and tapes, send in this card. And please visit our website at www.parallax.org.

Name _____

Address _____

City _____ State _____ Zip _____

Country _____

mind. I couldn't imagine what had caused such terrible nightmares.

A few days later I told some friends about these dreams. Gordon suggested a number of psychological explanations, but none of them fit the way I was feeling. Perhaps the dreams were an expression of all my recent anxieties, or perhaps they were no more than phantasms caused by the virus or a reaction to the medicine. Whatever the dreams may or may not have meant, I can't help feeling that they are somehow related to Ly's inscription. When the storm of destruction hits, I hope I am at home to face it with my friends. Heaven forbid that when I return, "the sky will be torn asunder," and I will only be able to find the ones I love "deep in my own heart."

Late last summer when I left the beautiful woods and the lake at Medford, I only had two days to visit Princeton before returning to New York. I'll never feel comfortable among the skyscrapers and busyness of New York, but there is always a good lecture or exhibit to attend, and many fine concerts, libraries, and museums of art and archeology.

My first impressions of New York came from an odd, unsettling encounter. Gordon drove me from Princeton to New York in his spacious car. I unloaded my luggage in my new room at Columbia and then we walked into town to shop for a few things. As we were walking down Amsterdam Avenue, a man, forty-ish and stylishly dressed, ran up to us. Speaking in a loud and overly familiar voice, as though he'd known us for years, he said to me, "What kind of get-up is that? Are you a Buddhist monk or something?"

Gordon answered for me, "Yes sir. That is correct."

Then, in an even louder and more presumptuous voice, the man asked where I was from. I answered Vietnam, but he appeared not to have heard of it. Then he asked, "Do Buddhists believe in Jesus?"

I replied, "Yes."

Surprised, he asked me to explain. I felt awkward standing in the middle of the sidewalk surrounded by crowded buildings. It was not an easy place to have such a discussion.

Gordon helped me out by saying, "What he says is true."

The man ignored Gordon and spoke directly to me, "In America, people say anything they want and attribute it to Jesus Christ. They sell God just to make a few dollars." Then he launched into a lengthy commentary on what he'd just said.

I asked him, "What path do you follow?"

He stopped to think and then pulled out his wallet, and said, "Here's my religion." I expected to see a church membership card, but he held a wad of one dollar bills and said, "This is the path I follow." His religion was money! Gordon and I began to laugh so hard that we cried. Then we bade the eccentric fellow farewell.

I said, "You have to admire his honesty. He said aloud things that others only think. You know, Gordon, he is the first New Yorker I've ever met."

We stopped at a dry cleaner's to see if they could re-dye my faded robe. The cost was so high, I hesitated. Then the proprietor told me, "In a few weeks you'll want to throw that costume out and start wearing Western clothes. People always come here dressed from their old country, but then they start wearing American clothes." I politely explained that this was not a costume, but a monk's robe, and that I had not just arrived in America. We thanked him and left.

That evening I persuaded Gordon to join me for dinner at the Vietnamese restaurant on Amsterdam Avenue. It's the only restaurant in New York that serves Vietnamese food. When I was still at Princeton, I saw an advertisement for it in a newspaper and wrote down the address. We had to walk past 121st Street before we found it. There were no customers when we entered. Two Vietnamese students who waited on tables were sitting at a table talking. They jumped up when they saw us and invited us to sit down at a corner table. They'd probably lived overseas most of their lives, because neither knew that I was a monk. The girl spoke fluent Vietnamese and asked if I was from Cambodia. I smiled and shook my head no. Gordon smiled, too. We ordered several dishes and asked the two young people to tell us about the restaurant. As we were leaving, I told them

that I was a monk from their homeland. They seemed
overjoyed and said that their families were Buddhist.
Later I learned that Mrs. Lan, the owner, considered her
restaurant to be a cultural institution. The food, art-
work, music, and interactions with waiters could help
increase their customers' understanding of and apprecia-
tion for Vietnam. It was very impressive. The waiters
spoke Vietnamese, English, and French, and could
converse knowledgeably about everything from cuisine
to politics. The young man I met that day also spoke
fluent German.

Those are the unforgettable memories of my first day
in New York. By the time I returned this fall, I'd become
used to city life, though my days in the woods at Medford did end all too soon! I am currently a teaching and
research assistant at Columbia. I teach five hours a week
and have office hours as well to meet with students and
assist them in their research, for which I receive $350 a
month, which makes me relatively "wealthy." I've become good friends with two of my students, David and
Steve. Steve and I appreciated each other from the
moment we met. When he suggested that we share an
apartment, I agreed. David frequently comes over and
joins us for meals. We usually stay up late discussing
many subjects in the pleasant atmosphere of our little
apartment.

Steve has joined me in eating only vegetarian food this
semester. I asked if it made him feel weak or tired, but

he said it didn't. "On the contrary," he said, "I feel much better." We always eat at home. We eat rice twice a day, using chopsticks. Steve is quite good at using them, because he lived in Japan one summer.

I feel as close to Steve as to Hung or Tue. Steve is the same height as I am — quite short for an American — and has light brown hair and a slightly pointed chin. His eyes are brown and he has the sensitive nature of an artist. He loves Eastern philosophy and is taking several Asian Studies courses including Chinese. It is moving to watch him write Chinese characters.

Steve confides his ups and downs to me, and I offer reflections that I hope are helpful. He sits and listens intently, sometimes wrinkling his eyebrows. Occasionally conflicts arise because of Steve's Western way of looking at things and my inability to express myself in ways other than Asian. But that's only natural. I think Steve has been influenced by Professor Cerbu's admonition, "Go East but stay West." My question is, If you stay West, how can you truly go East?

We rent our apartment for $150 a month. It has one bedroom, a study, a living room, a bathroom, and a kitchen. The address is 306 West 109th Street. We live on the fifth floor and have two large windows overlooking the street. To see the sky, you have to lean out the window. Steve brought all of the furniture, dishes, and kitchenware, so I haven't had to worry about a thing. Steve's father is the dean at a prestigious technology

institute. Steve is also gifted intellectually but has no
interest in science or technology. His mother came to
visit him a couple weeks ago and brought many delicious
foods.

I cook and wash the dishes. Steve does the shopping
and housecleaning. Because Steve spends a lot of time at
school, it is easier for me to assume the role of "home-
maker." I need to be on campus only a few hours a week.
I prefer to do research projects at home. I can work more
effectively here in our quiet apartment, and Steve is
happy to pick up whatever books I need at the library.
My library card entitles me to borrow dozens of books at
a time for two weeks each. It's a pleasure to cook for
Steve. He compliments everything I make. I think Steve
could be a vegetarian the rest of his life and not tire of it.
And I could cook for him forever and never feel my
efforts wasted.

In the beginning Steve didn't know how to shop for
the right ingredients. I took him to an Asian market
several times to show him what to buy there — shiitake
mushrooms, tofu, daikon, pickled cabbage, and other
uniquely Asian foods. He buys fresh vegetables from one
of the small grocers on Broadway. We also found a shop
that sells high quality rice in ten-pound bags. Most
Americans buy rice in tiny cardboard boxes. On the days
he gets out of class early, Steve shops on his way home.
Two bags of groceries fill the large refrigerator in our
apartment. Our kitchen is modern and very clean —

Steve scrubs it almost daily. The gas stove is most conve-
nient to use. Early each day, I prepare breakfast. Steve
stays up late and wakes up late, so he barely has time to
eat even a small breakfast before going out the door.
Some days I go with him to school in the morning, but I
come back home by eleven o'clock. Steve gets home at
12:30, famished, and we sit down to lunch. I always cook
enough for lunch and dinner, so I only need heat up
leftovers for the evening meal.

I prefer to stay in during the afternoon. I read, write,
prepare lessons, and answer letters. Sometimes David
comes to the apartment with Steve, and we eat dinner —
quietly and peacefully — in the living room. Steve and
David continue their conversation while I wash the
dishes. When I wash the dishes, I feel relaxed. The water
is warm and soothing. Sometimes I even play with the
soap bubbles and hum childhood songs. I wipe the stove
clean, put things away, and then take a hot shower,
change clothes, and join Steve and David. Such evenings
are delightful. Steve understands my nature, and so turns
off the electric lamps and lights candles for the softer
light. We don't talk all that much. We mostly just sit
there, each of us enjoying our own reflections. David
often stays late, and leaves only when I gently remind
him of the hour. At other times, the two young men go
off for the whole day, and I eat dinner alone.

Steve is a caring friend who listens deeply to my de-
scriptions about the situation in Vietnam. If it is possible,

he'd like to visit Vietnam some day. We've even talked
about him coming to stay at Phuong Boi. I've told him of
our love for Phuong Boi and how Phuong Boi is like a
spark of fire in each of our hearts that can never be
extinguished, the spiritual food that feeds our hopes and
dreams. Perhaps I've exaggerated, but Steve's eyes light
up every time he hears me mention Phuong Boi. He is
determined to learn Vietnamese, and I've begun teaching
him a few phrases. Steve has a passion for languages.
Even though he just began studying French, he is already writing poetry in French. At the Asian market, he
tries out his Chinese. Already, he can carry on a rudi-
mentary conversation. Steve likes my idea to create a
"village" when I return to Vietnam, where many of us
could live in community together, based on true fellow-
ship.

Steve takes care of all the heavy tasks. He knows that
I catch cold easily, so he insists on running all of the
errands. When I do come down with a cold or flu, he
spoons my back, and his strong hands soon chase away
the chills. When I don't improve, he calls Dr. Cushman.

Steve doesn't get along well with his parents. Last
summer he met a Japanese woman, and they've been
corresponding ever since. She has promised to visit him
this spring. Steve's family insisted he come home for the
holidays, although he wanted to be here in Princeton
with me. He took a plane home two days before I left
New York. Our apartment on 109th Street is now cold

and empty. The lights and heat are turned off. And here I am, sitting in the familiar lap of Princeton. It is twilight, and the snow continues to fall. I'll go find Saphir. We can cook a hot meal together and then watch the 7:00 news on the TV at the Campus Center.

Princeton, New Jersey

Today I received more than thirty letters, forwarded
from New York. The only ones from Vietnam were a
card from Hue Duong and a letter from Phuong. The
others were Christmas cards from American friends. In
America, people spend a fair amount of money sending
Christmas cards. Each family keeps a list of friends, and
then buys hundreds of cards, signs each one, places them
all in envelopes, and addresses and stamps each one. If
you send cards to only ten friends, you have time to
select a special card for each person. You even have time
to write ten short notes. But when your list includes
hundreds of friends and acquaintances, you have to buy
large boxes of identical cards and sign and address them
assembly-line style. What is most important, apparently,
is not to forget anyone. The list changes over the years
— one friend dies and another behaves poorly, so that
"diplomatic relations" are severed. And new friends are
added to the list. Some Americans assume I must be sad,
spending the holidays alone at Princeton. But I'm not sad
at all. In fact, I had to refuse several invitations to visit
friends' families so I could cherish this time for myself. It
is very peaceful and comfortable here. I think about

those people who are homeless and without heat, people who have little reason to celebrate.

In Vietnam, the war is escalating. Our people are caught between a hammer and an anvil. We've lost so much already. The country has been divided in two and engulfed in flames. Even Phuong Boi is fading into the fog. But as long as we have each other, we can never be truly alone. We want to stand with those who have been abandoned. I want others, at least occasionally, to turn their thoughts to those who suffer — to think about them but not pity them. Those who suffer do not want pity. They want love and respect.

During the Christmas season in America, many organizations make donations to those in need. People send contributions for orphans, widows, and the poor without ever seeing their faces. But a direct encounter is necessary to understand another's suffering. Only understanding leads to love. Huge sums of money and material goods are distributed to the poor during this season, but these gifts are largely the fruit of pity and not love. One organization distributes several thousand pairs of shoes to poor children. Among those who donate a few dollars to pay for a pair of shoes, I doubt that many actually envision the happiness on the face of the child when she receives the shoes, or even envision the shoes they are buying for her.

Last year at this time, I went shopping with Kenji, a young Japanese student. On Christmas Eve, the stores

were packed with last-minute shoppers, everyone rush-
ing about, anxious to get home on time for Christmas
get-togethers. Kenji and I had to buy enough food to
last a week, since the stores here are closed from Christmas until the first of the year. The sight of two young
Asians grocery-shopping on Christmas Eve moved
several people to pity. One woman asked if there was
something she could do to help us. We thanked her and
wished her a Merry Christmas. The checkout girl,
bright and cheery, looked at us warmly and wished us a
Merry Christmas. Everyone assumed we were lonely. It
was Christmas, and we were so far from home. But
since neither of us are Christian, we didn't have warm
memories of past Christmases to make us feel lonely. In
Saigon, pine boughs, Christmas cards, gold ribbons,
and other Christmas trappings do announce the season.
Even at Phuong Boi we celebrated Christmas Eve by
staying up late decorating a Christmas tree. But we
didn't experience the deep feelings our Christian friends
have. Perhaps it is because we respect Christ as a great
teacher but don't look on him as God. The same is true
of Buddha. We respect him as a great teacher, but we
don't worship him as a god. The holiday we feel most
enthusiastic about in Vietnam is Têt.

Still, when Christmas Eve arrived in Princeton, we
noticed how desolate Brown Hall felt. It was cold but
not snowing, so we decided to walk into town. We
strolled along the empty streets. All the houses and

stores were closed tight. Somehow, it evoked in me the
feeling of New Year's Eve back home and made me feel
homesick. We returned to Campus Center a bit melancholy, drank some tea, talked, and then watched TV. It's
funny how much our surroundings influence our emotions. Our joys and sorrows, likes and dislikes are col-
ored by our environment so much that often we just let
our surroundings dictate our course. We go along with
"public" feelings until we no longer even know our own
true aspirations. We become a stranger to ourselves,
molded entirely by society. Our friends at Phuong Boi
always stood up to social conformity and resisted
society's molds. Naturally, we met with opposition, both
internal and external. Sometimes I feel caught between
two opposing selves — the "false self" imposed by society and what I would call my "true self." How often we
confuse the two and assume society's mold to be our true
self. Battles between our two selves rarely result in a
peaceful reconciliation. Our mind becomes a battlefield
on which the Five Aggregates — the form, feelings,
perceptions, mental formations, and consciousness of our
being — are strewn about like debris in a hurricane.
Trees topple, branches snap, houses crash. These are our
loneliest moments. Yet every time we survive such a
storm, we grow a little. Without storms like these, I
would not be who I am today. But I rarely hear such a
storm coming until it is already upon me. It seems to
appear without warning, as though treading silently on

silk slippers. I know it must have been brewing a long
time, simmering in my own thoughts and mental formations, but when such a frenzied hurricane strikes, nothing outside can help. I am battered and torn apart, and I
am also saved.

I passed through such a storm this past autumn. It
began in October. At first it seemed like a passing cloud.
But after several hours, I began to feel my body turning
to smoke and floating away. I became a faint wisp of a
cloud. I had always thought of myself as a solid entity,
and suddenly I saw that I'm not solid at all. This wasn't
philosophical or even an enlightenment experience. It
was just an ordinary impression, completely ordinary. I
saw that the entity I had taken to be "me" was really a
fabrication. My true nature, I realized, was much more
real, both uglier and more beautiful than I could have
imagined.

The feeling began shortly before eleven o'clock at
night on October first. I was browsing on the eleventh
floor of Butler Library. I knew the library was about to
close, and I saw a book that concerned the area of my
research. I slid it off the shelf and held it in my two
hands. It was large and heavy. I read that it had been
published in 1892, and it was donated to the Columbia
Library the same year. On the back cover was a slip of
paper that recorded the names of borrowers and the
dates they took it out of the library. The first time it had
been borrowed was in 1915, the second time was in

1932. I would be the third. Can you imagine? I was only
the third borrower, on October 1, 1962. For seventy
years, only two other people had stood in the same spot I
now stood, pulled the book from the shelf, and decided
to check it out. I was overcome with the wish to meet
those two people. I don't know why, but I wanted to hug
them. But they had vanished, and I, too, I will soon
disappear. Two points on the same straight line will
never meet. I was able to encounter two people in space,
but not in time.

I stood quietly for a few minutes, holding the book in
my hands. Then I remembered what Anton Cerbu had
said the day before, when we were discussing how to
research Vietnamese Buddhism. He told me that I was
still young. I didn't believe him. I feel as though I've
lived a long time and have seen so much of life. I'm
almost thirty-six, which is not young. But that night,
while standing among the stacks at Butler Library, I saw
that I am neither young nor old, existent nor nonexist-
ent. My friends know I can be as playful and mischie-
vous as a child. I love to kid around and enter fully into
the game of life. I also know what it is to get angry. And
I know the pleasure of being praised. I am often on the
verge of tears or laughter. But beneath all of these emotions, what else is there? How can I touch it? If there
isn't anything, why would I be so certain that there is?

Still holding the book, I felt a glimmer of insight. I
understood that I am empty of ideals, hopes, viewpoints,

or allegiances. I have no promises to keep with others. In that moment, the sense of myself as an entity among other entities disappeared. I knew that this insight did not arise from disappointment, despair, fear, desire, or ignorance. A veil lifted silently and effortlessly. That is all. If you beat me, stone me, or even shoot me, everything that is considered to be "me" will disintegrate. Then, what is actually there will reveal itself — faint as smoke, elusive as emptiness, and yet neither smoke nor emptiness; neither ugly, nor not ugly; beautiful, yet not beautiful. It is like a shadow on a screen. At that moment, I had the deep feeling that I had *returned*. My clothes, my shoes, even the essence of my being had vanished, and I was carefree as a grasshopper pausing on a blade of grass. Like the grasshopper, I had no thoughts of the divine. The grasshopper's gods perceive form, sound, smell, taste, touch, and objects of mind. They know increasing and decreasing, defiled and immaculate, production and destruction. When a grasshopper sits on a blade of grass, he has no thought of separation, resistance, or blame. Human children prefer dragonflies whose wings and bellies are as red as chili peppers. But the green grasshopper blends completely with the green grass, and children rarely notice it. It neither retreats nor beckons. It knows nothing of philosophy or ideals. It is simply grateful for its ordinary life. Dash across the meadow, my dear friend, and greet yesterday's child. When you can't see me, you yourself will return. Even when your heart is filled with despair, you will find the same grasshopper on the same blade of grass.

Steve had left to spend a few days in Boston, and I was alone in our apartment. I left the bedroom door wide open day and night, like a prayer. What I was undergoing was neither happy nor sad. Some life dilemmas cannot be solved by study or rational thought. We just live with them, struggle with them, and become one with them. Such dilemmas are not in the realm of the intellect. They come from our feelings and our will, and they penetrate our subconscious and our body, down to the marrow of our bones. I became a battlefield. I couldn't know until the storm was over if I would survive, not in the sense of my physical life, but in the deeper sense of my core self. I experienced destruction upon destruction, and felt a tremendous longing for the presence of those I love, even though I knew that if they were present, I would have to chase them away or run away myself.

When the storm finally passed, layers of inner mortar lay crumbled. On the now deserted battlefield, a few sunbeams peeked through the horizon, too weak to offer any warmth to my weary soul. I was full of wounds, yet experienced an almost thrilling sense of aloneness. No one would recognize me in my new manifestation. No one close to me would know it was I. Friends want you to appear in the familiar form they know. They want you to remain intact, the same. But that isn't possible. How could we continue to live if we were changeless? To live, we must die every instant. We must perish again and again in the storms that make life possible. It would be better, I thought, if everyone cast me from their thoughts. I cannot be a human being and, at the same time, be an unchanging object of love or hatred, annoyance or devotion. I must continue to grow. As a child, I always outgrew the clothes my mother sewed for me. I can preserve those garments, fragrant with childish innocence and my mother's love, in a trunk for memory's sake. But I must have new, and different clothes now to fit who I have become. We must sew our own clothes and not just accept society's ready-made suit. The clothes I make for myself may not be stylish or even accepted. But it is more than a matter of clothes. It is a question of who I am as a person. I reject the yardstick others use to measure me. I have a yardstick of my own, one I've discovered myself, even if I find myself in opposition to public opinion. I must be who I am. I cannot force myself back into the shell I've just broken out of. This is a source of great loneliness for me. Perhaps I could persuade my dearest friends to accompany me on my voyage through space, but it might be dizzying for them, and might even incite feelings of hatred or resentment. Would they force me to return to earth, back to the illusory plane of old hopes, desires, and values, all in the name of friendship? What good would that be for any of us?

That is why I want to burn down the huts where my friends dwell. I want to incite chaos to help them break through the shells that confine them. I want to smash the chains that bind them and topple the gods that restrain them. For us to grow, petty amusements or even sorrows must not dominate us. A free person neither adheres to nor violates life's rules. The most glorious moment in life is to witness a friend's *return*, not exactly a return, but an infinitely exquisite moment when he emerges from the chaos caused by the annihilation of his last refuge. There he is, liberated from the hard shells of a thousand lifetimes, standing nobly in the brilliant light cast by his burning refuge. In that moment, he will lose everything, but in the same moment, he possesses everything. Beginning at that moment, we are truly present for each other.

During my struggle I was unable to converse, even after Steve returned. I could only manage manual chores. Steve recognized that I was undergoing something unusual and took great care not to disturb me. When I think of how sensitive he was during that time, great affection wells up in me. He didn't try to draw me into conversation. He only communicated what was essential. From time to time, I was aware that he was watching me, his eyes filled with concern. He spent time in the bedroom so I could have the front room to myself. He was so understanding. One Sunday morning I suggested we take a walk down to the river. We sat on the grass until early afternoon and then walked home. We didn't exchange a word the whole time. Back at the apartment, Steve asked, in a soft voice, "Are you tired, Thây?" I answered that I wasn't and thanked him.

Youth is a time for seeking truth. Years ago I wrote in my journal that even if it destroys you, you must hold to the truth. I knew early on that finding truth is not the same as finding happiness. You aspire to see the truth, but once you have seen it, you cannot avoid suffering. Otherwise, you've seen nothing at all. You are still hostage to arbitrary conventions set up by others. People judge themselves and each other based on standards that are not their own. In fact, such standards are mere wishful thinking, borrowed from public opinion and common viewpoints. One thing is judged as good and another as bad, one thing virtuous and another evil, one thing true and another false. But when the criteria used to arrive at such judgments are not your own, they are not the truth. Truth cannot be borrowed. It can only be experienced directly. The fruit of exploration, suffering, and the direct encounter between one's own spirit and reality — the reality of the present moment and the reality of ten thousand lifetimes. For each person, it is different. And it is different today than it was yesterday.

When we discover something to be true today through our own direct experience, we will see that our previous assumptions were wrong, or at least incomplete. Our new way of looking transcends yesterday's desire, prejudices, narrow-mindedness, and habits. We see that to

use the golden molds and emerald yardsticks of yesterday's understanding is nothing less than slavery or im-
prisonment. When we attain a new understanding of
reality, it is impossible to accept things we know to be
false. Our actions will be based on our own understanding, and we will follow only those rules we have tested
through our own direct experience. We will discard false
rules and conventions of the current social order. But we
have to expect that society will turn on us with a vengeance. Human history is filled with the tragedies caused
by that vengeance. History teaches that we die if we
oppose the system, yet many individuals continue to
challenge the darkness, despite the danger in doing so.
Those who pursue the truth are members of the community of truth seekers and reformers throughout time and
space. They do not resign themselves to a collective fate
that offers no laurels. The faint beams of light that appear after the desolation of the storm made me feel even
more alone and abandoned. I felt the unbearable pain of
a woman who is about to give birth to a child she already
knows will be sentenced to death. She is consumed by
despair, inconsolable and humiliated. She knows that she
is with child, but a child who is already condemned to
die. And she knows she will have to witness her child's
death. There is no way to avoid her fate. Why couldn't
she give birth to a healthy, sweet child like other mothers, a child who would give her hope, pride, and joy, a
child who would earn her the praises of others? But we

have to stand up for the truth. We cannot just gather moss like an old stone or assume a false self, once we see the truth.

There was a poor, young woman who dreamed of living in luxury, surrounded by jewels and silks. Then she met and married a wealthy widower, and her dream came true. She did not even mind that her husband had not married her for love. In fact, he married her because she looked exactly like his first wife. She agreed to dress, act, and speak like his first wife. At first, it wasn't a problem, but gradually it became quite oppressive. She was herself, yet she had to act like his first wife — to wear the colors she liked to wear, read the books she liked to read, and eat the foods she liked to eat. The young woman couldn't continue. It was suffocating. She was no more than a mannequin on which her husband hung his first wife's clothes and personality. But she didn't have the courage to give up the luxury she had become accustomed to. She was trapped by her own desires.

Anyone reading this story will want her to muster the strength needed to leave her husband and return to a simple country life where she can reclaim her true self. We think, "If I were in her place, that is what I would do." But we are only outside observers for whom the solution seems easy. If we were actually in her place, we would suffer the same confusion and indecision. Who among us would not? We already do the same thing. We feel forced to comply with the dehumanizing demands of society, and we bow our heads and obey. We eat, speak, think, and act according to society's dictates. We are not free to be ourselves, just as she was not free to be herself. We become cogs in the system, merchandise, not human beings. Our individuality is undermined, yet we comply because we lack the courage to refuse society's demands. We are no better than the wife of that man. We, too, have become so accustomed to our way of life with its conveniences and comforts that we allow ourselves to be colonized.

One day, she discovers that his first wife had been unfaithful to her husband. She takes this information to her husband in hopes he will come to his senses and let her be herself. But he tells her he knew about his first wife's infidelity, and because of that, he'd killed her. Her death, however, did not extinguish his anger. When he saw how closely she resembled his first wife, he married her and insisted she dress and act exactly like her. Now at last, she had become his first wife, and he could kill her again. He lunged at her, and she fought for her life.

I do not know whether she died or not. I leave the story unfinished. If she didn't, she certainly came close to the edge, like so many of us now. I hope humanity will awake in time and not wait, as she did, until the last moment to resist.

One morning I felt the sky brighten a little. I received a birthday card from home, which arrived exactly on my birthday. That was the day I felt myself reborn. In the card, Tue had copied three lines of a poem by Vu Tru:

> *Walking in the desolate desert*
> *a bear attacks me by surprise.*
> *I simply look him in the eye.*

Yes, I thought. I have looked the beast straight in the eye, and seen it for what it is. I am like someone just recovered from a near-fatal illness who has stared death in the face. I got dressed, walked outside, and strolled along Broadway, thirsty for the morning sun after so many days of darkness. The winds of the storm had finally dispersed.

Two days after my birthday, I went to a Buddhist
temple to pray for my mother. It was the full moon day
of October, which is the anniversary of my mother's
death. It was also the first day of a three-day celebration
the temple had organized to commemorate the seventieth anniversary of Buddhism in the United States.
About two hundred people were gathered, representing
many countries, although most were from Japan. It isn't
a large temple — the sanctuary is about the size of the
one in the An Quang Pagoda's Buddha Hall — but it
bears the illustrious name "American Buddhist Academy." Courses in Buddhist philosophy and practice are
offered, as well as classes in Japanese, tea ceremony,
and flower arranging. The temple belongs to the Japanese Pure Land Sect and is overseen by Hozen Seki, the
senior priest, and a Dr. Phillips, who used to be a professor at the University of Delaware.

There are about eighty thousand Buddhists in the
United States, mostly Chinese and Japanese. The Pure
Land Headquarters is in Washington, D.C. About seventy recently ordained Pure Land ministers, all Japanese, live throughout the United States. Some of them

also teach Japanese language and literature at American universities. Altogether there are fifty-four Pure Land temples, large and small. The one in New York is smaller than the one in Washington. At the ceremony, I met two Theravada monks in saffron robes, Venerable Anuruddha from Connecticut and Venerable Vinita from Massachusetts. The Sri Lankan ambassador, Mr. Susantha de Fonseka, was also there.

I strolled the five blocks from my apartment to the temple at 331 Riverside Drive, and arrived just in time for the sermon. I have to admit I didn't find the sermon very inspiring. Such sermons will hardly be effective in sowing seeds of Buddhism in America. The Pure Land sect emphasizes seeking salvation from what appears to be an external source. This approach is familiar to Europeans and Americans, who have plenty of seminaries and eloquent ministers to spread the word of Christian salvation. The Pure Land sect's efforts to look like Western churches seem to me to reflect their lack of understanding of the true American needs. Americans place a high value on independence. Their children are encouraged to be self-sufficient and self-reliant. A Buddhist approach that emphasizes self-effort and self-realization, like Zen, to build, develop, and awaken the individual, seems to be better suited to the American spirit. Christianity and Pure Land Buddhism have the appearance of considering that humans are too weak to achieve salvation without divine intervention. In fact, Zen is generating a lot of interest here. Professor D. T. Suzuki's voice has struck a chord across the country. People who live in a frenetic society, exhausted by interminable plans and thoughts, thirst for the serenity and self-contentment that a path like Zen offers.

Americans like to eat Japanese food, listen to koto music, attend tea ceremonies, and arrange flowers. After the sermon, there was a koto concert. To me, the koto player more than made up for the lackluster sermon. I sat between two Americans who looked rather distracted during the sermon, but obviously enjoyed the music.

I, too, enjoyed the music. The musician's name was Kimioto Eto, a young, around thirty-year-old man with a kind and open face. Dressed in a black kimono, he slowly mounted the stage, led by a young man gently guiding his arm. I wondered if he had poor eyesight. After Reverend Seki introduced him, Eto slowly sat down and smiled quietly. I was deeply touched by his presence. He never looked at the audience but settled his gaze on the podium that was draped with a white cloth. His smile was calm and composed. I never imagined a smile like that was possible in this country.

He said he wished to dedicate his playing to Kanzeon, the Bodhisattva of Compassion, to commemorate the seventieth anniversary of Buddhism in America. He explained that the number seven held deep personal significance for him. His father had died seven years ago, and his mother died seven months ago. His eyes filled with tears, and his quiet face was intense with feeling. I detected elements of faith, memory, and sorrow in his face. He played songs he had composed himself. The first was called "Song of Hope." Though the melody was tinged with sadness and yearning, it also expressed endurance and the will to move forward. The second piece, "Autumn Wind," was scented with the memory of loved ones, and the third, "Language of Faith," expressed his devotion to the Way of Compassion. Each piece was followed by a long pause during which I had the impression the audience stopped breathing and simply gazed at the young musician with the serene smile. At the end of the third piece, he mentioned that he was blind. Everyone seemed moved, and indeed, my whole being was touched. No one had guessed that he was blind.

I wanted to weep. I stood up and left, even though he had several more pieces to play. Three beautiful pieces were enough for me. I walked slowly along Riverside Drive, feeling rather melancholy. I could still see Kimioto's smile in my mind, so wondrously serene. No one could smile like that unless they had passed through great suffering. I understood why his smile had stirred me so deeply the moment I saw him.

Riverside Drive was abandoned, and I remembered the warnings of friends never to walk alone at night on an empty street. Like every city on earth, New York has its share of crime. I crossed 108th Street back to Broadway, and as I did, the moon came into view, as round as the Buddha's lotus-face. It appeared like magic in a sliver of sky, framed by the towering skyscrapers. It seemed as though the moon and I were traveling in the same direction.

The full moon of October. My mother was with me. No doubt she had followed me to the temple as the moon was first peeking over the horizon. As I listened to the sermon and then to Kimioto's music, the moon shone on the temple roof, and it followed me home. My mother died six years ago on the full moon day of October. The midnight moon is as gentle and wondrous as a mother's love. For the first four years after she died, I felt like an orphan. Then one night she came to me in a dream, and from that moment on, I no longer felt her death as a loss. I understood that she had never died, that my sorrow was based on illusion. She appeared in my dream on an April night when I was still living in the central highlands of Vietnam. She looked the same as always, and I spoke to her quite naturally, without a tinge of grief. I had dreamed about her many times before, but those dreams did not have the same impact on me as that night.

When I woke up my mind was at peace. I realized that my mother's birth and death were concepts, not truth. The reality of my mother was beyond birth or death. She did not exist because of birth, nor cease to exist because of death. I saw that being and nonbeing are not separate. Being can exist only in relation to nonbeing, and nonbeing can exist only in relation to being. Nothing can cease to be. Something cannot arise from nothing. This is not philosophy. I am only speaking the truth.

That night at about one a.m. I awoke, and my grief was gone. I saw that the idea that I had lost my mother was only an idea. Being able to see my mother in my dream, I realized that I could see my mother everywhere. When I stepped out into the garden flooded with soft moonlight, I experienced the light as my mother's presence. It was not just a thought. I could really see my mother everywhere, all the time.

In August, when I was still at Pomona, I wrote a small book entitled *A Rose for Your Pocket,* to help the young people back home appreciate the miracle of having a mother. As I wrote, the birds were singing in the forest. Only after I'd sent it off to Nhien did I realize that I had been writing from this new way of seeing. It was the way I described in my letter to Thây Thanh Tu. Whenever I teach Vietnamese literature, I always mention this couplet by Ly Dynasty Zen Master Thich Man Giac:

> *Do not say that when spring is gone,*
> *that there are no flowers left.*
> *Just last night, in the front yard,*
> *a plum branch bloomed in the middle of winter.*

I always admired the feeling of this poem, but I never fully understood Venerable Man Giac's meaning until that night when I began to see the true wonder of things, like perceiving a flowering plum branch on a dark winter's night.

In our time, the struggle between old and new will reach its crescendo. It's not over yet, and we carry scars of this struggle in our hearts. Questions raised by contemporary philosophers make us feel lost and anxious. Confused minds suggest that existence is meaningless, even absurd, and this adds another coat of black to our darkened hearts. "Existence is foul. Humans are loathsome. No one can hope to be good. There is no way to beautify life." Even while adopting such mindsets, people cling to the illusion that we are free to be who we want. Yet most of the time we are merely reacting to the wounds engraved on our hearts or acting out of our collective karma. Almost no one listens to his or her true self. But when we are not ourselves, any freedom we think we have is illusory. Sometimes we reject freedom because we fear it. Our true selves are buried beneath layers of moss and brick. We have to break through those layers and be liberated, but we are afraid it may break us, also. We have to remind ourselves over and over again that the layers of moss and brick are not our true selves.

When you realize that, you'll see every phenomenon,

every dharma, with new eyes. Begin by looking deeply at yourself and seeing how miraculous your body is. There is never any reason to look at your physical body with contempt or disregard. Don't ignore the very things that lie within your grasp. We don't value them. We even curse them. Consider your eyes. How can we take something as wonderful as our eyes for granted? Yet we do. We don't look deeply at these wonders. We ignore them, and, as a result, we lose them. It's as though our eyes don't exist. Only when we are struck blind do we realize how precious our eyes were, and then it's too late. A blind person who regains her sight understands the preciousness of her eyes. She has the capacity to live happily right here on earth. The world of form and color is a miracle that offers blissful joys every day. After we have this realization, we cannot look at the blue sky and the white clouds without smiling. The world constantly reveals its freshness and splendor. A blind person who regains her sight knows that paradise is right here, but before long she too will start to take it for granted again. Paradise comes to seem commonplace, and, in a matter of weeks or months, she'll lose the realization that she is in paradise. But when our "spiritual eyes" are opened, we never lose the ability to see the wonder of all dharmas, all things.

When I was a young monk I was taught that the greatest sufferings were birth, sickness, old age, death, unfulfilled dreams, separation from loved ones, and contact with those we despise. But the real suffering of human-kind lies in the way we look at reality. Look, and you will see that birth, old age, sickness, death, unfulfilled hopes, separation from loved ones, and contact with those we despise are also wonders in themselves. They are all precious aspects of existence. Without them, existence would not be possible. Most important is knowing how to ride the waves of impermanence, smiling as one who knows he has never been born and will never die.

The Buddha told this story: "A man threw a stone at a dog. Crazed with pain, the dog barked at the stone, not understanding that the cause of his pain was the man, not the stone." In the same way, we think that forms, sounds, smells, tastes, and objects of touch are the sources of our suffering, and that to overcome suffering, form, sound, smell, taste, and touch must all be destroyed. We don't realize that our suffering lies in the way we see and use form, sound, smell, taste, and touch, because we view reality through the dark curtains of our narrow views and selfish desires.

Here in America, I feel an intense longing for the familiar sound of Vietnamese. There are times I think, If I could only hear a familiar voice for two minutes, I could be happy all day long. One morning Phuong telephoned. It seemed completely natural to be talking to him. Though we didn't talk long, I was in good spirits the rest of the day.

Since then, whenever I talk with a friend, I listen with

all my attention to their words and the tone of their voice. As a result, I hear their worries, dreams, and hopes. It is not easy to listen so deeply that you understand everything the other person is trying to tell you. But every one of us can cultivate the capacity of listening deeply. I am no longer indifferent to phenomena that pass before my senses. A leaf, a child's voice — these are the treasures of life. I look and listen deeply in order to receive the messages these miracles convey. Separation from loved ones, disappointments, impatience with unpleasant things — all these are also constructive and wonderful. Who we are is, in part, a result of our unpleasant experiences. Deep looking allows us to see the wondrous elements contained in the weaknesses of others and ourselves, and these flowers of insight will never wilt. With insight, we see that the world of birth and death and the world of nirvana are the same. One night while practicing sitting meditation I felt the urge to shout, "The work of all the Buddhas has been completely fulfilled!"

It is not possible to judge any event as simply fortunate or unfortunate, good or bad. It is like the old story about the farmer and the horse.[1] You must travel throughout all

[1] One day a farmer went to the field and found that his horse had run away. The people in the village told the farmer it was, "Bad luck!" The next day the horse returned and the village people said, "That is good luck!" Then the farmer's son fell off the horse and broke his leg. The villagers told the farmer that this was bad luck. Soon after, a war broke out and young men from the village were being drafted. But because the farmer's son had a broken leg, he was not drafted. Now the village people told the farmer that his son's broken leg was really "good luck."

of time and space to know the true impact of any event. Every success contains some difficulties, and every failure contributes to increased wisdom or future success. Every event is both fortunate and unfortunate. Fortunate and unfortunate, good and bad, exist only in our perceptions.

People think it is impossible to establish a system of ethics without referring to good or evil. But clouds float, flowers bloom, and wind blows. What need have they for a distinction between good and evil? There are people who live like clouds, flowers, and wind, who don't think about morals, yet many people point to their actions and words as religious and ethical models, and they praise them as saints. These saints simply smile. If they revealed that they do not know what is good and what is evil, people would think they were crazy.

Who is the real poet? The sweet dew that a real poet drinks every day might poison others. For someone who has seen into the nature of things, knowledge gives rise to action. For those who have truly seen, there is no philosophy of action needed. There is no knowledge, attainment, or object of attainment. Life is lived just as the wind blows, clouds drift, and flowers bloom. When you know how to fly you don't need a street map. Your language is the language of clouds, wind, and flowers. If asked a philosophical question, you might answer with a poem, or ask, "Have you had your breakfast? Then please wash your bowl." Or point to the mountain forest.

If you don't believe me, look and see.
Autumn has arrived.
Scattered leaves of many colors flood the mountain forest!

If they still cannot see, you might pick up a stick and threaten to strike them in order to get them to stop using concepts to try to understand the truth. If there had been a poet like that living in Phuong Boi, the mountain forest would have been even more radiant.

In Buddhist sutras, there is a term that is translated as "adornment." I'm reminded of the time King Hue Tong of the Ly Dynasty invited Zen Master Hien Quang to leave his meditation hut to come dwell in the palace. Hien Quang refused, saying that the talented and virtuous Zen masters already living in the capital had more than "adorned" the palace. The presence of a realized person beautifies life by their path of non-action. What does a path of non-action have to do with plans and programs?

In fifteen minutes, it will be midnight. Christmas is almost here. I am awake in this sacred hour writing in my journal. My thoughts flow, and it feels wonderful to pour them onto paper. I've written about the spiritual experience that revealed to me how to look and listen with full attention. Such moments might only come once in a lifetime. They appear as ambassadors of truth, messengers from reality. If we're not mindful, they may pass unnoticed. The secret of Zen masters is discovering the path of return to such moments, and knowing how to pave the way for such moments to arise. The masters know how to use the dazzling light of those moments to illuminate the journey of return, the journey that begins from nowhere and has no destination. Quach Thoai's poem describes the appearance of a dahlia:

> *Standing quietly by the fence,*
> *you smile your wondrous smile.*
> *I am speechless, and my senses are filled*
> *by the sounds of your beautiful song,*
> *beginningless and endless.*
> *I bow deeply to you.*

Do you see? The moment appeared. The curtain was drawn back for a second, and the poet could see. The dahlia is so commonplace that most people do not truly see it. When you can hear its eternal song and see its miraculous smile, it is no longer an ordinary flower. It is an ambassador from the cosmos.

Tru Vu wrote:

> *The petal of a flower is made only of four elements,*
> *but it emits a spiritual perfume.*
> *Your eyes are made only of the four elements,*
> *but they radiate the energy of love.*

Tru Vu was expressing his sudden surprise. The

moment arrived in a flash of light, and then it vanished.
Being able to see just once in a lifetime is no small ac-
complishment. If you've seen once, you can see forever.
The question is whether you have the determination and
diligence. Many young people today feel trapped in
prisons of discouragement and self-hatred. They regard
reality as meaningless, and they treat themselves as
despicable beings. My heart opens to them. Caught in
despair, they seek liberation through destructive means.
It would be wonderful if we could identify and dissolve
the sources of such a dark view of life.

If you tarnish your perceptions by holding on to suffering that isn't really there, you create even greater
misunderstanding. Reality is neither pleasant nor unpleasant in and of itself. It is only pleasant or unpleasant
as experienced by us, through our perceptions. This is
not to deny that earthquakes, plagues, wars, old age,
sickness, and death exist. But their nature is not suffering. We can limit the impact of these tragedies but never
do away with them completely. That would be like wanting to have light without darkness, tallness without
shortness, birth without death, one without many. One-
sided perceptions like these create our world of suffering. We are like an artist who is frightened by his own
drawing of a ghost. Our creations become real to us and
even haunt us.

The night of November 2nd is one I will never forget.
It was a moonless, cloudless night, and the sky was filled

with stars, each as bright as a child's eyes. In fact, that
was the sky in my mind. The actual night was windy and
rainy. The windows in my room were shut tight, and I
was unable to sleep. I had been reading Bonhoeffer's
account of his final days, and I was awakened to the
starry sky that dwells in each of us. I felt a surge of joy,
accompanied by the faith that I could endure even
greater suffering than I had thought possible. Bonhoeffer was the drop that made my cup overflow, the last
link in a long chain, the breeze that nudged the ripened
fruit to fall. After experiencing such a night, I will never
complain about life again. My heart was overflowing
with love. Courage and strength swelled in me, and I
saw my mind and heart as flowers. All feelings, passions,
and sufferings revealed themselves as wonders, yet I
remained grounded in my body. Some people might call
such an experience "religious," but what I felt was totally
and utterly human. I knew in that moment that there
was no enlightenment outside of my own mind and the
cells of my body. Life is miraculous, even in its suffering.
Without suffering, life would not be possible. There is
nothing permanent, and there is no separate self. Neither
is there impermanence or no-self. When we see life
deeply, there is no death. Therefore, it isn't necessary to
say "everlasting life."

For the next month I meditated on the bodhisattvas
described in the *Lotus* and other *Prajñaparamita Sutras*.
These beings are so beautiful, it is easy to understand

how their presence beautifies the many Buddha Lands. But why confine their beauty to Buddha Lands? How about right here on earth? The presence of bodhisattvas is enough to transform the earth into a Buddha Land. Who can say that this earth is not a Buddha Land? The pole that we raise every year at Tết expresses the realization that this very earth is a Buddha Land.

Sometimes healthy, energetic bodhisattvas, like Never-Disparaging Bodhisattva and Earth-Holding Bodhisattva, wear ragged clothes. Earth-Holding devotes himself to rebuilding roads and bridges in order to restore communication and contact. In today's world, there are countless broken bridges and innumerable Earth-Holdings devoting their bodies and minds to rebuilding bridges of communication and understanding among individuals, nations, and cultures. Wherever Never-Disparaging Bodhisattva goes, he offers words of encouragement: "You have the strength to go forward. Believe in yourself. Don't succumb to low self-esteem or passivity. You will become a Buddha." His message is one of confidence and self-determination. I think about the peasants in the countryside of all the poor countries of the world. Do they have someone to encourage them to believe in their own abilities so they can build a future that they, as much as anyone else, have a right to? Our world needs millions more bodhisattvas like Never-Disparaging.

We can rejoice that our world does have many bodhisattvas who can be found on every path of return, sowing seeds of faith, resolve, and confidence. Kwan Yin, for example, always finds ways to be with those who are suffering. She fears nothing, and uses whatever means are appropriate to the circumstance. She takes on whatever form is needed — monk, politician, merchant, scholar, woman, child, god, or demon. Can we listen deeply like Kwan Yin? Using every form and means possible, in the spirit of Kwan Yin, we will bring help to our world. The wholehearted spirits of bodhisattvas like Never-Disparaging and Earth-Holding will rebuild our world. Let us not forget Kshitigarbha, the Earth-Store Bodhisattva. He makes the vow to be with those who are in the places of greatest suffering. As long as any being remains in hell, Kshitigarbha will be there. His spirit is irrepressible. Wherever such persons are found, flowers blossom, even in the depths of hell.

Bodhisattvas are frequently shown wearing beautiful garments. Shining gems adorn their heads, arms, and necks. Monks, on the other hand, are never portrayed in fancy dress. The bodhisattva image is meant to symbolize how bodhisattvas beautify and adorn life. Their presence makes life beautiful. Artists portray them in clothes as colorful as children's New Year's outfits, as bright as an early spring day. No one sees the existence of suffering more deeply than a bodhisattva, yet no one maintains as refreshing and unwavering a smile. I can hear the bodhisattvas saying, "We are not here to weep and wail, we are here to make life beautiful." We must thank these friends and we should wear our finest clothes, too, to help them adorn life. They will delight to hear us calling them our friends. We needn't think of them as remote beings on pedestals. We can recognize their presence every day among those we see. It is not arrogance that allows us to approach them as friends. It is freedom from the rigid ideas that have encased us. O Oriole, though your throat is tiny, sing out, and let your song praise life's wonders! Kwan Yin's necklace of jewels is sparkling, and so is your song. Let the morning sun roll down the hills like a golden stream, and let all the flowers bloom as one until they cover the meadows, welcoming the miracle of mindfulness.

That wondrous night my mind and heart opened like a flower, and I perceived all the bodhisattvas as dear friends helping us right here and now in this very life, and not just as remote deities. This same insight is expressed in a daily gatha:

> *When the lotus blooms,*
> *we see the Buddha immediately*
> *and touch the reality of no-birth and no-death.*
> *All bodhisattvas become our companions.*

Once our minds and hearts have opened like flowers, they will never fade. They will be like the lotus flowers in the Pure Land. The light shed by lotus blossoms will show us where to find our friends along the path.

At midnight, while the snow was quietly drifting down, I put on a warm coat and walked to the Campus Center. I sat down beside Ralph Nelson who was watching a Christmas special on TV. Ralph's family lives in the South, and it is too far for him to travel for a holiday visit. I had the distinct feeling he was homesick. He'd driven to Pennsylvania the day before yesterday to visit a friend, and on the drive back to Princeton he got caught in a blizzard and had to pull his car over to the side of the road and sleep right there. It can be dangerous to be caught in such a situation. The temperatures can drop so severely that even someone inside a closed car could freeze to death. Luckily Ralph survived the ordeal and made it back safely to campus. I asked him, "Are you sad to be apart from your family on Christmas Eve?"

He answered, "I'm used to living alone. It's no big deal."

I detected some sadness in his eyes. Just then a funny movie came on, and Ralph and I laughed together until 1:30. When we left the Campus Center, the snow was up to our knees. I bade Ralph good night and turned toward Brown Hall. When I got back to my room, I changed into a dry pair of socks and warmed my feet by the heater.

Last year I spent Christmas Day in the countryside, where I experienced the warm spirit of American families celebrating the holiday. Christmas here is very much like Tết. Young and old all give and receive lots of presents.

I was asked by a young boy, "Do Buddhists celebrate Christmas?"

I replied, "Yes. In my country, Buddhists celebrate Christmas on the full moon day of the fourth month. We call it 'Buddha-mas.'"

As I was warming my feet, I thought about the young campers at Cherokee Village, and I slept very soundly.

20 January 1963
New York City

During the last days of the lunar year, the markets in Saigon are bustling with merchants and shoppers. I can visualize the towering mounds of watermelons, bright green on the outside and red as rubies inside. In the U.S., it is nearly impossible to find a watermelon at this time of year. Otherwise, I would buy several and carve them into lanterns. Yesterday I received a package from Vietnam filled with New Year's presents — sandalwood, white candles, a tin of tea, candied ginger and fruits, and watermelon seeds. I was so happy! Like a man of leisure I boiled water for tea, lit a candle, and cracked the watermelon seeds between my teeth. Steve does not care for watermelon seeds, or to say it more accurately, does not understand the important function they provide. He doesn't like candied ginger either. He took a small bite, wrinkled his nose, and declared it too hot. He was able to enjoy the tea and some of the candied fruit.

Steve asked me what benefits watermelon seeds could possibly confer. There are many benefits, I replied. Americans enjoy their favorite foods to celebrate weddings, birthdays, Thanksgiving, and other special occasions, yet they never say that they "eat the holiday." In

Vietnamese, we say *"an Têt,"* which means "We eat the
New Year." We also eat birthdays, weddings, a baby's
first-month celebration, a person's sixtieth birthday, and
even someone's memorial. The three days of Têt require
constant eating. Wherever you go, you are obliged to eat
something or you might offend your host. Thanks to the
custom of serving watermelon seeds, we can eat continu-
ously without getting stuffed. The second benefit is that
no matter how many watermelon seeds you eat, you
don't have to worry about harming your health. If you
eat too much of other foods, you'll get a stomachache.
But watermelon seeds never cause problems. The third
benefit is that while your mouth is occupied cracking
and chewing the seeds, you are not expected to talk.
That is especially useful when you don't have much to
say. That leads to the fourth benefit. By avoiding speaking, you don't have to worry about saying something
you'll later regret. Watermelon seeds teach people how
to take the time to reflect until they have something
useful to say. In Vietnamese, we say, "You can always
learn from others, whether they are five years old or
eighty." Watermelon seeds have played their part in
promoting mindful speech in people of all ages. When
you have nothing constructive to say, you simply use
your teeth to break open the seeds, while listening intently. If you know nothing about a subject, no one will
criticize you if you quietly chew your seeds. Steve could
not stop laughing as I explained these benefits of water-

melon seeds. He suggested that I write a book on the subject.

In Vietnam, it is now springtime. Here it is still freezing cold, and winter will drag on for at least two more months. The pine trees covering the hills around Tu Hieu Pagoda are glistening with needle buds. Pines there always look tall and erect at New Year's. Many friends must be strolling among those pines, breaking branches to bring home a New Year's gift from the Three Jewels. The pines suffer a lot at this time of year. The beautiful temple grounds look bare and ragged after people have gathered armfuls of branches. One year I heard that Xa Loi Temple planted a grove of pines just for people to gather branches, in order to protect the other trees. I don't know if their plan worked or not. I suspect people considered the cultivated branches less "authentic" and not as capable of emitting "Buddha-spirit" as the other trees. The practice of breaking branches to bring home ceases to be a lovely custom when trees are being damaged.

Dharma talks and ceremonies attended by large crowds at the New Year serve a purpose, but I hope serene temple settings will also be preserved. It is good when a person has the opportunity to enter a small, quiet space in order to have a personal contact with the Buddha. Small, quiet spaces are more conducive for spiritual experiences. In such a space, meeting the Buddha becomes an encounter with your own true self.

Nowadays, people build large temples to hold prayer services. Although that is valuable, I also long to preserve individual meetings between teacher and student in which the student enjoys the teacher's complete attention, the kind of attention that calls forth the student's mindfulness. The teacher also benefits from a student who is completely present. When the Buddha lifted a flower at Vulture Peak, only Mahakashyapa smiled. Vulture Peak itself and the entire assembly sitting there disappeared, and only two people were truly present, the Buddha and Mahakashyapa. That was a true encounter.

One afternoon while strolling back to my temple, I passed a group of young Buddhists returning from the pine-covered hills of Tu Hieu. Some were on foot, others on bicycle. Each of them carried a pine branch, and I could feel the tree's pain. I am sure this Têt will be no different. I hope my friends will do their best to protect the pine trees.

When it is midnight in Vietnam, it is noon here in New York, so I plan to celebrate Têt at noon. Last year at Princeton, I welcomed the New Year at noon with a Vietnamese young man who lived nearby. It was a different time, place, and climate, but the same celebration. Everyone in Princeton had left for work or school, unaware that people in Vietnam were celebrating Têt. But I was aware. I knew that Têt had arrived. It is a matter of awareness. If you are not aware of something, it does not exist. The subject and the object of awareness are not separate.

One day I went to Butler Library to find a particular philosophy book. When I entered the philosophy room, there were only two elderly men sitting at a table, reading. I found the book I wanted, a volume by a Professor Schneider. I read for awhile, I'm not sure how long exactly. Then suddenly, I was startled by the distinct aroma of a grapefruit blossom. I was astonished. There are no grapefruit trees growing for more than a thousand miles. I've been away from home so long that the slightest sound or smell of Vietnam is very precious to me.

> *Jasmine, lily, ngau,*
> *none compares to the lingering perfume*
> *of the sweet grapefruit blossom.*

Grapefruit is the fragrance of my home and of many folk songs. I put down my book. It was impossible to read. After thinking about it, I reasoned that the fragrance could not be real, that it could not be emanating from an actual plant. It must have been my imagination, some memory that had floated up from my subconscious mind. I have had similar experiences in the past. I quieted my mind and returned to Professor Schneider. But there it was again, the unmistakable fragrance of grapefruit blossoms. Perhaps a young woman had entered the

room unnoticed wearing grapefruit-scented perfume. I
don't know if such perfume exists, but it seemed a plau-
sible explanation. I stared at my book, imagining a re-
fined and graceful young woman, perhaps from Vietnam,
or at least from Asia. I felt the urge to look up and see if
she was really there, but I resisted. I was afraid that
instead of seeing a modest young woman from Asia, I
would see a brash woman heavily made-up, and I didn't
want to be disappointed. So I sat there for five minutes,
afraid to look up and unable to read.

As a novice I was required to read Buddhist philosophy. I was only sixteen and unable to grasp concepts like
Interdependent Co-Arising, and Oneness of Subject and
Object. It was difficult to understand why the perceiver
could not exist independently from the object being
perceived. I managed to get a high mark on my philosophy exams, but I didn't really understand. I reasoned
that, thanks to awareness, the finite world of phenomena
could partake of the transcendent realm of consciousness. Being can only be defined in opposition to nonbeing, and if there is no awareness of either being or
nonbeing, it is as though nothing exists. The deeper
implications were not at all clear.

As I write these lines, no one else has read them yet.
These lines that contain my thoughts, feelings, paper,
ink, time, space, and handwriting, as well as all the other
phenomena that have contributed to their existence,
exist only in my consciousness. Readers who may one

day read these lines also lie within my consciousness. All phenomena — Vietnam with her flowering grapefruit and orange trees, graceful coconut trees, and towering areca palms, and the lively city of New York, with its sun, snow, clouds, moon, and stars — lie within my own consciousness. They are merely concepts. My world, including all my friends and readers, all the grapefruit and starfruit trees I have ever touched or thought about, is a world of concepts. When you read these lines, will you see me in them? This city as well as my thoughts and feelings will then become concepts in your consciousness. For you, these concepts are not the result of direct contact with the objects of my consciousness. Void of physical reality, these concepts are shared through the medium of consciousness. The physical basis of consciousness, both personal and collective, has disappeared.

In the conceptual world, subject and object are two sides of the same coin. This became clear to me late one night less than two years ago, when I was staying at Bamboo Forest Temple. I awoke at 2:30 a.m. and could not get back to sleep. I lay quietly until I heard the first bell. Then I sat up and tried to locate my slippers with my feet, but they must have been too far beneath the bed. So I walked to the window barefoot. The cool floor beneath my feet felt totally refreshing and invigorating. I leaned against the windowsill and peered outside. It was still too dark to see anything, but I knew that the plants in the garden were still there — the oleander bush still stood in the same corner and the wildflowers still grew beneath the window. I experienced how the subject of awareness cannot exist apart from the object of awareness. The oleander and the wildflowers were the objects of consciousness. Subject and object of consciousness cannot exist apart from each other. Without an object, the subject cannot be aware of anything. Mountains and rivers, earth and sun, all lie within the heart of consciousness. When that realization arises, time and space dissolve. Cause and effect, birth and death, all vanish. Though we dwell a hundred thousand light years from a star, we can cross that distance in a flash. The saints of the past can return to the present in a microsecond, their presence as vivid as a bright flame.

I stood by the window and smiled. Someone seeing me grinning like that might have thought me deranged. The curtain of night was totally black, but not without meaning. This was infinitely clear in my consciousness. All of miraculous existence was illuminated by that smile.

You are there, because I am here. We inter-are. If we do not exist, nothing exists. Subject and object, host and guest, are part of each other. I knew that when morning came, I would not find anything new or unusual about the visible world. The blue sky in the west and the pink horizon in the east exist only in my consciousness. Blue does not have a separate life, nor does pink. They are only blue and pink in my consciousness. It is the same with birth and death, same and different, coming and going. These are all images in our consciousness. If you look into my eyes, you will see yourself. If you are radiant, my eyes will be radiant. If you are miraculous, my consciousness will be miraculous. If you are distant and remote, I will be distant and remote. Look into my eyes and you will know if your universe is bright or dark, infinite or finite, mortal or immortal. The poet Tru Vu wrote:

> *Because eyes see the blue sky,*
> *eyes glisten sky-blue.*
> *Because eyes see the vast ocean,*
> *eyes extend as far as the sea.*

As my smile flashed in the dark night, I felt as gentle as a cloud, as light as a feather floating on a stream of cool water, my head held by the little waves. Looking up, I saw the blue sky and white clouds that had passed during the day. The clouds were still white, the sky was still blue, perhaps even whiter and more blue. Is that not a sign of the birthless and deathless nature of reality? I heard the autumn leaves rustling in the forest, grasses in the fields.

Then I spotted a star in the sky and immediately returned to the place where I was standing, my feet touching the cool floor and my hands resting on the windowsill. "I am here," the star said. "Because I exist, the universe exists. Because I exist, you exist. Because I exist, the pebbles and the distant clouds exist. If all of these don't truly exist, how can I? The existence of a speck of dust makes everything else possible. If dust does not exist, neither does the universe, nor you, nor I."

I am happy to be on this earth. The river reflects everything in herself. Thanks to the river's flow, the flux of life is possible. And death lies within life, because without death there could be no life. Let us welcome the flow. Let us welcome impermanence and non-self. Thanks to impermanence and non-self, we have the beautiful world praised by Zen poets — the sheen of banana trees, the tall and perfumed areca trees reaching to the sun. The earth is filled with dust. Our eyes are filled with dust. There is no need to seek a Pure Land somewhere else. We only need lift our heads and see the moon and the stars. The essential quality is awareness. If we open our eyes, we will see. I am sure that heaven has areca, starfruit, lime, and grapefruit trees. I laugh when I think how I once sought paradise as a realm outside of the world of birth and death. It is right in the world of birth and death that the miraculous truth is revealed.

Vietnam has extraordinary rainstorms. One day, I sat by the window of a friend's home and watched a scene I could have watched forever. Across the street was a low-roofed dry goods store. Coils of rope and barbed wire, pots and pans hung from the eaves. Hundreds of items

were on display — fish sauce and bean sauce, candles
and peanut candy. The store was so packed and dimly
lit, it was difficult to distinguish one object from another
as the rainstorm darkened the street. A young boy, no
more than five or six, wearing a simple pair of shorts, his
skin darkened by hours of play in the sun, sat on a little
stool on the front step of the store. He was eating a bowl
of rice, protected by the overhang. Rain ran off the roof
making puddles in front of where he sat. He held his
rice bowl in one hand and his chopsticks in the other,
and he ate slowly, his eyes riveted on the stream of
water pouring from the roof. Large drops exploded into
bubbles on the surface of a puddle. Though I was across
the street, I could tell that his rice was mixed with pieces
of duck egg and sprinkled with fish sauce. He raised his
chopsticks slowly to his mouth, savoring each small
mouthful. He gazed at the rain and appeared to be
utterly content, the very image of well-being. I could feel
his heart beating. His lungs, stomach, liver, and all his
organs were working in perfect harmony. If he had had
a toothache, he could not have been enjoying the effort-
less peace of that moment. I looked at him as one might
admire a perfect jewel, a flower, or a sunrise. Truth and
paradise revealed themselves. I was completely absorbed by his image. He seemed to be a divine being, a
young god embodying the bliss of well-being with every
glance of his eyes and every bite of rice he took. He was
completely free of worry or anxiety. He had no thought

of being poor. He did not compare his simple black shorts to the fancy clothes of other children. He did not feel sad because he had no shoes. He did not mind that he sat on a hard stool rather than a cushioned chair. He felt no longing. He was completely at peace in the moment. Just by watching him, the same well-being flooded my body.

A violet shadow flitted across the street. The boy looked up for an instant, his eyes startled by the blur of bright color, and then he returned his gaze to the water bubbles dancing on the puddle. He chewed his rice and egg carefully, and watched the rain in delight. He paid no more attention to the passersby, two young women dressed in red and purple *ao ðai,* carrying umbrellas. Suddenly he turned his head and looked down the street. He smiled and became so absorbed in something new, I turned to look down the street myself. Two young children were pulling a third child in a wooden wagon. The three did not have a stitch of clothing on and were having a grand time splashing in the puddles. The wheels of the wagon spun round and round, spraying water whenever the wagon hit a puddle. I looked back at the boy on the doorstep. He had stopped eating to watch the other children. His eyes sparkled. I believe my eyes reflected his in that moment, and I shared his delight. Perhaps my delight was not as great as his, or perhaps it was even greater because I was so aware of being happy.

Then I heard him call out, "Coming, Mama," and he

stood up and went back into the shop. I guessed his mother had called him back in to refill his rice bowl, but he did not come out again. Perhaps he was now eating with his parents, who scolded him for dawdling so long over his first bowl. If that was the case, poor child! His parents did not know he had just been in paradise. They did not know that when the mind divides reality up, when it judges and discriminates, it kills paradise. Please do not scold the sunlight. Do not chastise the clear stream or the little birds of spring.

How can you enter paradise unless you become like a little child? You can't see reality with eyes that discriminate or base all their understanding on concepts. As I write these lines, I long to return to the innocence of childhood. I want to play the Vietnamese children's game of examining the whorls of a friend's hair — "one whorl your allegiance is with your father, two whorls with your mother, three whorls with your aunt, many whorls with your country." I'd love to make a snowball and hurl it all the way back to Vietnam.

In former days, my friends and I wanted to become heroes who could "shatter misfortune and level calamity." We did not know what it takes to become a hero, so we tried to imitate the knights of old. I cannot help smiling when I think of our youthful dreams. We hardly looked the part of brave knights as we clutched our bamboo swords and repeated the words of the ancients. Now as I write, surrounded by a cold and bustling city,

I feel a bit of the old desire. The world is the same as
when we were children, still patiently awaiting the appearance of real heroes.

Before the knights of old descended their mountain
training grounds to rescue those in need, they trained a
long time with revered masters in the martial arts. My
training as a Buddhist novice consisted of one small
book, *Gathas for Daily Life*. I learned to cook, sweep,
carry water, and chop wood. Some of us did not have
enough time to learn the arts of cooking, sweeping,
carrying water, and chopping wood before being forced
to descend the mountain. Others descended of their own
will before they were ready. With our talents and abilities still undeveloped, how could we save others? We
may have thought of ourselves as heroic, indispensable,
and may even have called ourselves heroes, but society
too often accepts those who are heroes in appearance
only, making it possible for such people to think they are
true heroes. They come to believe that if they were not
present, everything would fall apart. And yet when my
friends and I left Phuong Boi, the world did not disintegrate.

Life waits patiently for true heroes. It is dangerous
when those aspiring to be heroes cannot wait until they
find themselves. When aspiring heroes have not found
themselves, they are tempted to borrow the world's
weapons — money, fame, and power — to fight their
battles. These weapons cannot protect the inner life of

the hero. To cope with his fears and insecurities, the premature hero has to stay busy all the time. The destructive capacity of nonstop busyness rivals nuclear weapons and is as addictive as opium. It empties the life of the spirit. False heroes find it easier to make war than deal with the emptiness in their own souls. They may complain about never having time to rest, but the truth is, if they were given time to rest, they would not know what to do. People today do not know how to rest. They fill their free time with countless diversions. People cannot tolerate even a few minutes of unoccupied time. They have to turn on the TV or pick up a newspaper, reading anything at all, even the advertisements. They constantly need something to look at, listen to, or talk about, all to keep the emptiness inside from rearing its terrifying head.

When I was a child, I read a funny story about a man who always boasted to his friends about his brave exploits. But at home he was so afraid of his wife, he did not dare look at her crosswise. Present-day heroes are like that. They think they are real heroes because they are so busy, but if we could see their inner lives, we would see desolation. Present-day heroes descend the mountain intending to transform life, but are instead overcome by life. Without fierce resolve and a mature spiritual life, private demons cannot be controlled.

Gathas for Daily Life was a warrior's manual on strategy. As novices, we were handed it when we entered the monastery and instructed to keep it close at hand at all times, even to use it as a pillow at night. The verses in it taught us how to stay present with our own minds in order to observe ourselves throughout the ordinary actions of daily life: eating, drinking, walking, standing, lying down, and working. It was as difficult as trying to find a stray water buffalo by following its zigzagging tracks. It is not easy to follow the path of return to your own mind. The mind is like a monkey swinging from branch to branch. It is not easy to catch a monkey. You have to be quick and smart, able to guess which branch the monkey will swing to next. It would be easy to shoot it, but the object here is not to kill, threaten, or coerce the monkey. The object is to know where it will go next in order to be with it. That thin book of daily verses provided us with strategies. The verses were simple, yet remarkably effective. They taught us how to observe and master all the actions of body, speech, and mind. For instance, when we washed our hands, we said to ourselves:

> *Washing my hands in clear water,*
> *I pray that all people have pure hands*
> *to receive and care for the truth.*

The use of such *gathas* encourages clarity and mindfulness, making even the most ordinary tasks sacred.

Going to the bathroom, taking out the garbage, and chopping wood become acts infused with poetry and art.

Even if you have the perseverance to sit for nine years facing a wall, sitting is only one part of Zen. While cooking, washing dishes, sweeping, carrying water, or chopping wood, you dwell deeply in the present moment. We don't cook in order to have food to eat. We don't wash dishes to have clean dishes. We cook to cook, and we wash dishes to wash dishes. The purpose is not to get these chores out of the way in order to do something more meaningful. Washing the dishes and cooking are themselves the path to Buddhahood. Buddhahood does not come from long hours of sitting. The practice of Zen is to eat, breathe, cook, carry water, and scrub the toilet—to infuse every act of body, speech, and mind— with mindfulness, to illuminate every leaf and pebble, every heap of garbage, every path that leads to our mind's return home. Only a person who has grasped the art of cooking, washing dishes, sweeping, and chopping wood, someone who is able to laugh at the world's weapons of money, fame, and power, can hope to descend the mountain as a hero. A hero like that will traverse the waves of success and failure without rising or sinking. In fact, few people will recognize him as a hero at all.

The first delicate signs of spring are now revealing themselves in Vietnam. No matter how much further my homeland plunges into grief and sorrow, spring will always return with her message of hope. Spring always gives us faith to carry on. There is no sign of green here. Snow is drifting outside my window. But spring will come and the bare trees and the lawns now buried beneath the snow will once again wear the tender green garments of a prosperous spring.

Vietnam
1964 — 1966

I miss my time in New York. Steve and I shared so many joys and sorrows, I can never forget our time together. Our apartment on 109th Street has been rented to someone else now. Steve didn't mention it when I left, but I knew he wouldn't be able to afford the rent and utilities on his own.

As I write, I am in a small building made of thatched coconut-palm leaves. Coconut palms line the streams and marshes throughout South Vietnam. The walls of this building are coated with a mixture of mud and straw. Steve has never seen walls like this. The builders stripped bamboo canes, sharpened both ends, and then arranged them into lattices around four posts. They tied the canes in place with bamboo twine. Mud was then mixed with straw and spread over the lattices, filling every nook and cranny. I asked the builders to add a little cement to the mixture to make it sturdier. Once the bamboo lattice walls were covered, a final layer of mud was added and smoothed over. The mud turns chalky white when it dries and is quite attractive. The afternoon winds here can get gusty, but this cozy thatched building keeps the winds out.

It is early morning and I'm sitting by the window looking out at the rice fields brushed by the rising sun. To the left, a young girl is standing in the fields. Straight ahead, lush coconut palms line the damp arroyo. To the right extends the village. I see the water buffalo pens on higher, drier ground. The soil here is high in alum, and the river turns salty during the dry season. The absence of decent drinking water during the dry season can become a desperate problem.

Saigon is only ten kilometers away, yet it is so peaceful and quiet here. I returned from Saigon late yesterday after teaching a class. By the time I reached the village bridge, the full moon was peeking out over the coconut trees along the river. The breeze was so refreshing as I leisurely walked into the village. Villages like this are still relatively safe from the war. My sleep was only occasionally disturbed by sounds of distant gunfire.

This village is the site for an experimental development project my friends and I initiated right after I returned to Vietnam. We call it a "self-help village," and it will serve as a model for the kind of community Steve and I used to talk about. The name "self-help village" conveys the idea that this is a village where citizens share collective responsibility to develop the local economy and provide for education and health care. We want to uproot old attitudes of passivity — waiting for someone else to make a difference. We have recruited friends with organizational skills who are willing to learn the challenges of rural life by actually living here among the people. We hope their presence and know-how will catalyze a spirit of self-determination among those who live here. The villagers have accepted us as family. The building I am staying in has four rooms — three belong to the village school and one serves as a clinic. This building was planned and constructed by the villagers, with the encouragement and assistance of our friends. At present two of our friends, Tam Quang and Tam Thai, live here full-time. The rest of us return as often as we can. We learn from the villagers and try to test our ideas with their support. We have another ex-perimental village in nearby Thao Dien.

I know Steve would like it here, but it is not the right time for him to come. He has to finish his studies in the U.S. He was considering transferring to Saigon Univer-sity to deepen his understanding of Vietnamese culture, but I feel it is essential for him to stay at Columbia and complete his degree there. The situation in Vietnam is far more complex than Steve and I imagined when we dis-cussed our plans back in New York. The truth is that the presence of an American in one of our villages would hamper our efforts. My friends and I need to deepen our understanding of the current situation.

I arrived at Tan Son Nhat Airport in Saigon on a balmy afternoon. The flight was scheduled to make a stopover in Bangkok, but thick fog prevented us from landing there, so the pilot flew directly to Saigon. When

the plane landed and the engines quieted, I felt butter-
flies in my stomach. Phuong Boi was only two hundred
kilometers away. Just four hours by car to reach the
mountain forest, cradled in soft clouds, that protected
and nourished us for so many months.

After nearly three years overseas, I was home at last. I
felt restored by familiar sights, but I saw for the first
time on the ride into town just how undeveloped my
homeland is. We passed rows of low-roofed dwellings
packed with people and old, hunched men pedaling
pedicabs. I saw one old man, his back bared by a torn
shirt, barely keeping his ancient cab moving. He had no
customer, so he pedaled with only one foot, shifting his
weight from side to side to relieve his aching muscles.
Then a customer hailed him, and he braked and let the
man climb into the cab. The old man sat upright and
pedaled quickly. Barefoot, naked children played in the
streets amidst piles of garbage, sugarcane-juice vendors,
and motorcycles whose motors sounded like wounded
animals.

We entered Saigon. Several American-style highrise
apartments rose haphazardly along the streets. Crowds
of refugees from the countryside had poured into the
city to escape the war. I was unsettled by these sights
and recognized that Vietnam had entered a dire stage in
her history. Would my friends and I be able to do anything to help our people chart a new course?

That night I met with several young friends at Bam-

boo Forest Temple. Hearing their sad accounts of recent
events, I felt disheartened. The military had not made
use of the rising tide of public sentiment to help lead the
country forward. High-ranking Buddhist monks were so
blinded by the respect and admiration people gave them
that they had fallen into a state of complacency. The
very practice of Buddhism was endangered — a threat
that escaped most people's notice. Intellectuals and
students, aware of the potential of Buddhist teaching to
encourage and unite the people, had approached the
monks, but were disappointed by their complacency. At
the same time, they saw ambitious politicians flock to the
monasteries to seek the monks' support. Intellectuals
and students became increasingly disillusioned with the
Buddhist hierarchy. Vietnamese Buddhism, two thousand years old, was not offering a way out of the noose
that was strangling Vietnamese society.

I listened to my friends most of the night. I did my
best to comfort them and told them not to be discour-
aged. Our numbers might be small, I said, but our hearts
are strong. We must be like the yeast that leavens the
dough. We shared our hopes and our fears. I had had
similar gatherings with Vietnamese friends in Paris for
several days before returning to Vietnam, and so I was
exhausted. I slept all the next day and night, clear
through to the following morning. When at last I awoke,
Toan prepared breakfast for me.

That afternoon I strolled the grounds of Bamboo

Forest Temple with Toan and listened to him describe the projects our friends had organized in my absence. That night we held a second meeting in order to establish principles and objectives for our work.

The following morning (January 27, 1964) I traveled alone to Phuong Boi carrying nothing but a small knapsack. I caught a bus and felt relieved to get out of the city. We passed forests and rubber-tree farms. After a stop in Dinh Quan, we rode through mountain gorges until at last the forest of B'su Danglu emerged. Towering Dai Lao Mountain greeted me. I asked the driver to let me off along Highway 190, and then, throwing the knapsack over my shoulder, I walked slowly up the old road.

I passed Uncle Dai Ha's rubber-tree orchards and turned off the main road into the forest. There was no one in sight. Uncle Dai Ha's farm seemed deserted. I wondered if he and his family had moved to town to be safer. As I passed by his home, I glanced in the kitchen window. A pot of cold rice and a clutter of bowls sat on the table. Perhaps Uncle Dai Ha had hired a few laborers to watch the house and gardens. Perhaps I could find them. I cupped my hands to my mouth and called out several times, but there was no response. I crossed the second slope. The once-familiar path was completely overgrown and strangely deserted. Even the forest had become secretive and menacing.

I passed through the trees and began to climb the final

slope. Plum Bridge came into view. Several of its wooden planks were broken, so I had to step carefully. On the other side of the bridge was the path leading to Joy of Meditation Hut. I was surprised to find it as charming and inviting as it had been three years ago. Someone had been tending it. Who, I wondered, as I followed the path. At the spot where the path veers, I looked up and was flabbergasted to see Nguyen Hung standing by Joy of Meditation Hut holding a sickle and looking down at me. Nguyen Hung in the flesh! He recognized me the exact instant I recognized him. We cried out each other's name and ran toward each other, meeting halfway on the slope.

I asked Hung what he was doing at Phuong Boi. Hadn't he been in Dalat? He told me that he headed straight for Phuong Boi after receiving news of my arrival in Saigon. He knew that despite anyone's warnings, I would make my way to Phuong Boi. It was a joyous reunion, one that took me completely by surprise, even though we had long ago promised to meet each other again here.

It turned out that Hung had arrived the day before and cleared the paths leading from Plum Bridge to the main house and Joy of Meditation Hut. He wanted to minimize the shock for me of seeing the rundown and abandoned condition of Phuong Boi. He was hard at work clearing brush around Joy of Meditation Hut when he saw me below.

Montagnard House had burned to the ground in an accident — some Montagnard farmers were burning forest land to plant crops and the fire spread. We climbed Montagnard Hill and surveyed the scattered piles of ash and charred wood. Our hearts felt heavy. Ashes were all that remained of the beautiful place where we had spent so many peaceful hours. "When peace returns," I declared, "we will rebuild Montagnard House." Hung nodded in agreement. We walked back down the hill and visited all the old places. Phuong Boi did not disappoint us. Three fiery red roses bloomed on the rosebush as if to herald our return. The mimosa tree at the corner of the main house had grown tall and was vibrantly green. The pines I had planted were tall and healthy.

We made our way slowly to Meditation Forest. The sign that announced "Dai Lao Mountain, Phuong Boi Hermitage" was still there. The characters were not faded or dull. It was amazing paint that did not peel after six years. I bent down to pick up a pine cone and was met by the fragrance of *chieu* blossoms. We picked an armful of the snow-white flowers to offer on the Buddha's altar, which was in a pitiful state. No one had tended it for some time, and it was covered with dust and leaves.

We swept the altar with a broken branch and offered the flowers before the faded ink painting of the Buddha. Phuong Boi had been vacant for too long. The doors and windows had been purposely left unlocked to prevent intruders from breaking them. We knelt silently for a long time in the meditation room and then walked out, gently closing the door behind us. Phuong Boi's "Golden Age" was over. The New Year's Eve bonfires atop Montagnard Hill, the hikes for which we outfitted ourselves like warriors, the evenings of reciting poetry or discussing the challenges of the spirit and society were all gone. Hung and I did not speak.

There was graffiti scrawled in black coal on the walls, slogans from both warring parties. Hung told me that there'd been a fierce exchange of gunfire by Plum Bridge which left several corpses on the ground. Other skirmishes followed and Uncle Dai Ha decided to move his family into town. The only people who stayed on in the nearby strategic hamlet were families too poor to abandon the meager plots of land they'd been given.

Phuong Boi was abandoned. Our books and furniture had been moved to Dai Ha Hamlet. We could see signs that others had lit fires and spent nights in the main house. I later wrote to Steve and told him to give up his dream of coming to live with us at Phuong Boi. The days of Phuong Boi were over. Phuong Boi is scarred by war, empty and miserable. In the misty mornings and pristine evenings, Phuong Boi has become an abandoned nest. The birds have all flown away. They want to return, but the winds and rains prevent them from doing so.

Hung and I sat by the pond and talked until dusk. Though there were no signs of danger, we both felt uneasy. Hung counseled that we should walk back down to

Dai Ha Hamlet before dark. We shared the sweet rice cakes wrapped in my knapsack as we walked down the mountain. At Dai Ha, we caught a bus to Bao Loc, where we spent the night before returning to Saigon the next morning.

Our longing for Phuong Boi was so great that several of us returned for another visit a few months later, only to be arrested by government soldiers. We were released after several hours, but we did not dare visit Phuong Boi again. Silently, Phuong Boi endures alone. Countless other abandoned villages, mountains, and rivers silently endure the war. The war grows more violent every day. There is not a creature alive that does not long for its end. The war is wounding the earth and everyone's heart. Even the image of Phuong Boi that remains in our hearts has become a wound.

I will be at the self-help village all day. Because it is Sunday, the village school, called *Rossignol* (Mountain Bird Song), is closed. The village clinic is named Love Clinic. Today I'll join the other volunteers to learn more about the needs of the villagers. We are deeply committed to these projects, to find effective and suitable means to bring about rural development. The future of Vietnam depends on efforts like these to improve village life. Independence and sovereignty will only be assured when Vietnam is able to stand on her own. We must move toward a stable and self-sufficient economy.

Vietnam is not resource-poor. In both the lowlands

and highlands, we have many resources waiting to be developed. We must devote great effort to developing our agricultural resources. Technology that is just beginning to be developed depends on natural resources. In order for Vietnamese industry to move beyond its first tentative steps, we need to use our own raw materials and consume the products manufactured by our own industries. Only in that way can we avoid spending capital on foreign goods that could better be invested in developing new Vietnamese industries. We need to learn to use technology and effective market practices in developing agriculture. Agricultural progress cannot be separated from issues of health care, education, and self-governance. Real progress requires understanding and effort by all the people.

For decades, peasants have heard endless promises from politicians, but their lives have not changed. And now the war has destroyed their rice paddies and robbed them of their livelihoods and safety. The economy grows weaker every day. American aid is keeping the economy from completely falling apart, but in the process it is making Vietnam ever more dependent. The war has destroyed many things, including our country's ability to stand on her own feet economically.

I remember the discussions Steve and I had about the difficulties in East-West dialogue. I often found it difficult to express my thoughts and feelings in a way that Steve could grasp. The French lived side by side with

Vietnamese for nearly a hundred years. There was even a special school, The French Institute of the Far East, where students studied the history and culture of Vietnam, and yet French understanding of Vietnamese culture remained superficial. How can Americans, in a far shorter time span, hope to understand better? Americans put their faith in statistics and technical projects, but their ways do not work here. Methods that work in villages here are entirely different from methods taught in the Western universities. Papers, studies, and statistics are cited to justify spending money on projects that have no chance of success here. Vietnamese government officials, from top ministers down to minor officials, are only concerned about lining their own pockets. They don't even care if their corruption is exposed.

I wrote to Steve to try to help him understand the situation. I explained how years of unfulfilled pledges by President Diem had made the peasants mistrust all sugarcoated promises. They have been used and manipulated so many times, they mistrust and fear any government cadre sent to "assist" them. They know that most government employees become "soldiers in the war on poverty" only to get a good salary themselves. These government workers come dressed like slick urbanites and spend a few hours in a rural village or strategic hamlet, and all they do during these hours is spread government propaganda. They are completely out of touch and have no real desire to serve others. Their words and actions only offend. Some of them even flash guns and shoot at birds to instill fear in the people. Yet they themselves are too afraid to spend the night in the countryside. The Liberation-Front cadres conduct themselves more wisely. They wear simple black clothes like the peasants and share the "Three Togethers" with the people: eating, living, and working. They cook, sweep, wash dishes, and harvest rice alongside the peasants. They stay overnight and discuss concerns. The government is losing ground daily in the battle against the National Liberation Front.

American advisors place a great deal of faith in strategic hamlets, but they make sense in theory only. In actual practice, they destroy everything. Americans place too much trust in the power of money, and Mr. Diem places too much trust in the power of tyranny. The real reason for organizing strategic hamlets is to gather people into central locations where they can be "defended," which means controlled, to prevent infiltration from the other side. Areas under suspicion are the first to be organized into strategic hamlets. One day, villagers are ordered to leave their homes, forbidden to take any belongings with them. Soldiers gather the young and old, male and female, and lead them to a certain sector, where they are given a small plot of land, materials to build a hut, and money to live on until the first crops are ready to harvest. Soldiers burn the old village to the ground in order to destroy any hidden weapon caches or other links to the liberation fighters. The villagers are horrified when they see their ancestral homes go up in flames, and they shout in protest. Every peasant's home holds objects that, though simple, are irreplaceable—incense bowls, funeral tablets, wills, and cherished letters from loved ones. How can money replace such things? The people stagger to their new location, forced to take orders from government cadres and "start a new life." They've been robbed and humiliated.

The theory is that the villagers are now "safe." Members of the Viet Cong, however, are not so easily duped. They do not go around wearing uniforms. They enter the hamlets and live alongside the other villagers. Then one morning someone discovers a "mine" in the village assembly hall. It is only a fake, but it bears the emblem of the Viet Cong. The barbed wire surrounding the hamlet ceases to have any meaning. The fake mine serves as a powerful threat, "We are here, so take heed." The hamlet's false sense of security unravels. How can you win a war with bullets when you do not even know where the front line is?

Strategic hamlets are created to serve a political agenda, not a social one. That is why the people ignore the government's propaganda about wanting to improve the peasants' standard of living. My friends and I are convinced that a movement to rebuild our country must be based on an entirely different foundation. We want to

initiate a war on poverty, ignorance, disease, and misunderstanding.

We have two experimental villages in the south and
two in central Vietnam, in Khanh Hoa and Thuc Thien.
At first, the villagers looked at us with suspicion. They
kept their distance, remaining as cold as stones. Any
attempts to persuade them of our motives would have
been useless. They had already been through too many
"social revolutions." We did our best to be humble and
patient, and after awhile, their attitudes toward us
began to change. When they returned our smiles with
sincere smiles of their own, we were greatly encouraged. They began to open up to us and participate in
the projects we were doing on our own, such as trying
to create a simple school for the children. By gradually
winning their acceptance, we knew our efforts would be
a hundred times more effective. Once they began working with us to plan and carry out projects that would
improve and develop the village, we understood how
capable these people are. The people in small country
hamlets throughout Vietnam are the country's greatest,
untapped resource.

But Vietnam has become divided. The war has destroyed trust, hope, and all the constructive efforts of
the past. People are suspicious of every act of goodwill
and every promise made. Religion is the only institution
left that can inspire unity and social responsibility. We

must use the resources of our spiritual traditions to
bring about change. Buddhism has much to contribute
to this work, but we cannot wait for the religious hierarchy to act. They are reluctant to bring about change,
and they've repeatedly rejected our efforts to create an
engaged Buddhism. Our proposals lie in unopened
folders on their desks, gathering dust. Therefore my
friends and I will rely on our own resources to win, first,
the support of the people and, eventually, the support of
the Buddhist hierarchy. Gaining the people's understanding and support is paramount.

We now have an infrastructure of volunteers who can
help develop self-help villages. They are equally knowl-
edgeable about social concerns and religious teaching,
and they understand effective methods to combat poverty, disease, ignorance, and misunderstanding. They do
not work for wages or power, but with love and awareness. The spirit of self-help motivates them. These are
young people, like Steve and Nguyen Hung, who are
peace-loving and faithful and reject a life based on
materialism. They seek only the happiness that a life of
service can bring. They have the right kind of spirit to
succeed.

Vietnam does not lack such young people. There are
tens of thousands, perhaps hundreds of thousands of
them. Their eyes shine with faith. In a few months we
will open the School of Youth for Social Service, a new

kind of university that will train community development workers. The staff is made up of able, young
people, all anxious to get started. We have no money,
but we have a plan, goodwill, and lots of energy.

20 March 1964
Saigon

Steve's telegram came as a shock. Professor Anton
Cerbu has died. I never guessed we would lose such a
good friend so soon. I was very busy when I left New
York and only had time to telephone him to say good-bye.
He said he hoped the situation in Vietnam would improve
soon, so that I could return to New York and complete
the project we'd discussed so often — to start a Department of Vietnamese Studies at Columbia. The idea appealed to me, because it would be another way of serving
my homeland. There are already Departments of Japanese, Chinese, and Korean Studies at Columbia, and
interest is now turning toward Vietnam. I recall Anton's
animated face and bright eyes whenever we discussed this
plan. Now Anton is gone, and our Department of Vietnamese Studies will not happen. We have lost a pillar of
support. Anton had studied at the Institute of Oriental
Languages in Paris and was able to read Vietnamese. I
enjoyed his youthful, easy-going nature. As I sit here, his
image comes clearly to mind. Anton has died, leaving
behind so much unfinished work — research papers,
drafts, and documents yet to be published. I wonder if

anyone will go through his papers and prepare them for publication.

In December, shortly before I left New York, Anton counseled me to stay in the States. He said the time was not yet right for me to return, that I wouldn't find the necessary support for my ideas in Saigon. In the end, the call of Phuong Boi and my friends prevailed. I wasn't worried about Anton's health, because he had seemed so animated after his surgery. I even had to persuade him to rest from talking. I was afraid he would exhaust himself. On that same visit, Anton lent me his copy of *Studies on the Literature of Ancient Vietnam*, by Nguyen Dong Chi. I promised him, during our last telephone conversation, that I would return to New York "in a few years." Now he has departed. I know how much Steve and all his students loved him. A dozen of them pledged to donate blood the day he entered the hospital.

With spring just around the corner, why was Anton in such a hurry? Couldn't he have waited for the blossoms to appear on the branches? Perhaps winter was too long for him. And there were so many changes this past year. I think about Steve and can well imagine his face when he received the telephone call from the Cerbu family that Anton had died. The surgery was not successful. I am sure everyone in the Asian Studies Department mourns his death. Miriam will probably send me a letter soon.

Although Professor Cerbu is gone, I am confident that Steve will continue the path he has begun. I counseled him not to abandon his studies of Sanskrit and Chinese. Someday he and I will work together. I don't want Anton's death to discourage Steve. I am still here, and I will continue writing to Steve regularly.

I've been wanting to ask Steve, Where do you eat now, and who does the cooking? I cook only occasionally here, because there are so many other things to do. Hung and I share a small living space and eat our meals together. Hung is a talented cook, so I have grown lazy. I know I shouldn't, but Hung hasn't complained! Hung has grown up so much in the past three years, but he still likes to joke around. His antics actually provide a lot of relief. It is difficult to convey how difficult things are here in Vietnam.

Three Phuong Boi birds — Hung, Phu, and Man — have joined our new efforts. Ly lives nearby, but he is very busy putting out a newspaper and he has little time for much else. He still wears the brown peasant shirt he used to wear at Phuong Boi. Once in a while he does stop by, but he never stays longer than the time it takes to smoke half a cigarette. His newspaper was shut down by the authorities a week ago, but Ly refuses to submit. In the current political climate, no independent newspaper lasts long, regardless of how many readers it has. From time to time, Ly asks if I need money. I tell him that even without money, I am not poor. I paraphrase a haiku by Basho and tell him that even though the electricity has been shut off, the moon still shines in my window. Ly laughs and pulls a few bills from his pocket, which he insists is money he owes me for printing a recent article I'd written in his paper. I never know which article he is referring to, but I don't refuse his gesture.

Hung and I are temporarily staying at Van Hanh University. This Buddhist university is so new that it has not yet had time to construct any buildings. Several inner city temples have lent it space for offices and class-rooms. Our "apartment" is on the second floor of Phap Hoi Temple, in a poor, flood-prone neighborhood in Saigon. Phap Hoi Temple also serves as Van Hanh University's central office.

Van Hanh is an unusual university. It bears none of the distinguished marks normally associated with institu-tions of higher learning. When it rains, students have to wade through puddles to get to class, winding their way through the crowded market stalls — selling everything from dried fish to sweet potatoes — that line the en-trance to Phap Hoi Temple. The rector's living quarters and office comprise three tiny rooms, nothing like the fine accommodations of the rector of Hue University. But this location has its conveniences. In the mornings, we only need to step outside the door to buy breakfast, thus avoiding having to cook. For a few piasters, we can get a generous serving of sweet rice and beans wrapped in a banana leaf. We simply provide the chopsticks and *voilà*, breakfast is served. The same few piasters could also purchase boiled sweet potatoes, still steaming in their skins. And each morning, the temple caretaker provides us with a large pot of tea to accompany our breakfast.

Everyone rises early here, not like in New York, where people go to bed late and wake up late. Since the temple is adjacent to a monastery, we wake up at the sound of the first bell and the monks chanting. As dawn breaks, I open my window, which faces the alley. At that hour the streetlights cast a dim light, and the earliest vendors have already come and gone. Beneath one light pole against the temple wall stands the *hu tieu* woman. *Hu tieu* is a noodle soup, served with fresh bean sprouts, that is very popular in the south. Auntie (I call her that because I don't know her name) cooks a great kettle of broth at night. She must have to wake up at three a.m. to reheat it before carrying her wares on a yoke to market. The broth needs to be kept very hot, and so she carries it inside a coal-burning pot. She lifts the lid only when ladling the broth into a customer's bowl.

Every morning when I look down and see her preparing noodle soup, I am filled with an inexplicable feeling of peace. Her customers include Uncle Seven from the other side of the street, who prefers a bowl of *hu tieu* to bread dipped in a cup of *café au lait* before he departs for work, the woman who sells roasted corn on the cob and wearies of her own corn for breakfast, schoolchildren who are treated to bowls by their mothers or older sisters, and the housewife who fills her rattan basket with market purchases. In the alley market near Phap Hoi Temple, vendors of hot foods and vendors of cold foods jostle for space. Then they buy each other's offerings, because they do not consider their own dishes special.

Auntie's guests sit on low stools set before a large wooden tray, about a meter long, that she leaves leaning against the wall of the temple every day when she packs up and leaves. I guess her tray is never stolen because it's so old and beaten up. Or perhaps Auntie has an agreement with Uncle Liu, who sells Chinese herbs close by, to keep an eye on it for her. In either case, the tray leans against the temple wall rain or shine, every season of the year. The amount her customers pay determines what size bowl they get. Her prices are most reasonable. One piaster buys a small rice-bowl size serving, and three or five piasters buy a larger size. Some customers buy two or three bowls, one after the other. Auntie places lettuce, bean sprouts, and noodles into each bowl before ladling the hot broth. She uses her left hand to lift the lid of the steaming pot and holds the large ladle in her right. Even for the smallest bowl, she ladles twice. The first scoop is mostly clear broth, the second scoop always includes one or two pieces of meat. Even the one-piaster bowl receives a tiny morsel of meat. If extra pieces of meat swim into the second ladle, she returns them to the pot with a flick of her wrist. Her careful apportioning of ingredients reminds me of when I used to cook soup for 100 monks in the monastery. Fifty bowls had to be served from each copper kettle, and I had to be sure that every serving received a fair share of vegetables and broth. The task was complicated by the fact that I cooked different kinds of soup — jackfruit, greens, or mushroom soup. Mushrooms grown in Hue are famous for making a sweet broth. Once when I was short on greens but had a few mushrooms, I prepared a soup with both, adding two small tomatoes as well. The result was very watery. The tomatoes had dissolved, and there was only a speck of greens in each bowl, with hardly a mushroom in sight. Still the monks said the soup was delicious. I guess the mushrooms gave the broth some of that famous Hue flavor.

When Auntie finishes ladling the broth, she sprinkles fish sauce and fresh herbs into the bowl and sets it on the tray. Then she wipes a pair of chopsticks with the clean cloth that hangs on her carrying yoke, and hands them to the customer. She washes the bowls and chopsticks in a dishpan, dries them, and stacks them in a basket for her next customers. The rising sun brightens the alley. Later, when I take a break from my morning writing, I look out the window, and Auntie is gone. Her noodle soup sells out quickly every morning. I only saw her packing up once and that was at 8:30 a.m. She wiped everything clean, leaned her tray against the temple wall, and lifted the yoke across her shoulders. Most of the other vendors do not pack up until 10:30 or 11:00.

I imagine that Auntie has several school-aged children. She not only has to feed them but provide for their school supplies and tuition, in addition to her other household expenses. Can selling noodle soup bring in enough money? Perhaps she has another job in the afternoons. One thing is certain. She has to stay up late at night cooking her broth and rise early in the morning to bring it to market. Phap Hoi Alley market would be a sadder place without Auntie Hu Tieu and the other vendors. The women who sell vegetables, fish, and meat provide for their families' needs. There is also a woman who sells fabric, and a fellow who sells aluminum pots and pans by the entrance to Van Hanh University. He takes up about eight meters square. His pots gleam in the sunlight, and the great assortment of kitchen knives he displays are almost too bright to look at. Sometimes his display takes up so much space that it blocks the narrow gateway the university's car uses to enter and exit the temple grounds. The driver has to persuade Mr. Pots and Pans to move his shiny wares to one side. Of course, most of the vendors are quite understanding and readily move their wares out of the way whenever they see the car.

Six months ago, as a founder and director of Van Hanh University, I had several conversations with the university rector. He said, "This alley market is an embarrassment to the university. Let me get it cleared away.

None of the vendors has a proper permit. Once they are gone, I'll ask the Department of Public Works to come with bulldozers and fill in the potholes. Then the entrance to our university will look respectable."

He urged me to agree to his plan, but I refused. Finally I convinced him not to be so callous. The university, I explained, had not yet shown what benefits it might bring to the people. His plan would put a hundred people out of work and earn the university the hatred of the entire neighborhood. I thought of Auntie Hu Tieu and knew I could never support the rector's plan to make the school look more "respectable."

One day we received a delegation of Saigon's intellectual elite and members of the diplomatic corps. Saigon, a city of two-and-a-half million people, is known as the "Jewel of the Far East." But we still had almost no equipment, even chairs, and the rector had to borrow chairs from a number of furniture retailers he knew. The day before the visit, we made a special arrangement with the alley vendors not to spread their wares before the front gate. But the morning the delegation arrived, it was raining so hard that our distinguished guests had to tiptoe around huge puddles to enter the gate. As I welcomed them, I apologized for the puddles, but they just laughed.

Afterwards the rector whispered to me, "I see that you did not require bulldozers from Public Works to take care of the 'puddles.'"

I replied, "I only took care of them temporarily. They will be back."

The rector laughed also.

On moonlit nights, the narrow alleyway of Phap Hoi is as festive as Tết. The rising moon flickers through the long, graceful leaves of the areca palms, each four or five meters high, that line both sides of the alley. A vendor of toys sells his wares beneath a street lamp. Carts offer cool drinks. It is too hot to stay indoors, so families spread rice mats or pull chairs outside their front doors. Several of them carry on a little business at the same time. Some inflate rubber balloons to sell. They buy multicolored balloons wholesale, and then set up a small coal-burning stove outside, spread out a mat, and get to work. The heat softens the rubber, making it easier to inflate the balloons.

Adults sit and chat, while children run and play on these festival-like evenings in Phap Hoi Alley. Beneath the carefree surface, however, lie many hardships. The disruptive, eroding influence of the war is making life more and more difficult for these families. Refugees are pouring into poor neighborhoods like these. The streets are filled with pale and thin children. I don't know why, but I find these children beautiful, even the poorest among them. They don't have the rosy cheeks and robust health of children from well-off families, but they are beautiful in their own way. I think all children are

naturally beautiful. But perhaps I've paid more attention to these children in recent months, and so I am able
to appreciate deeply their beauty.

Truc Lam Temple
Go Vap, Gia Dinh Province

I received a long letter from Steve several weeks ago, but I've been too busy to answer it until today. There has been massive flooding in central Vietnam, the worst in sixty years. The last time it flooded like this was also a Year of the Dragon. I've just returned from a relief mission with three young workers. While there, I was able to see my teacher in my root temple. He just turned eighty, and, like other elders in this region, recalls the terrible flood sixty years ago. This year, thousands of people drowned and tens of thousands lost their homes and possessions. There has been a tremendous outpouring of support from the South. I cannot begin to count the number of organizations that have contributed. The School of Youth for Social Service collected truckloads of food, medicine, and clothing, and we organized a team to deliver the supplies directly to the victims. This is dangerous work, because the flooded areas are in some of the areas of heaviest fighting. Your life can be taken at any moment by a bomb or a sudden firefight. But our hearts compel us to go to the victims in these forbidden zones.

I feel for Steve. He is tired of New York and doesn't want to live there anymore. If he can stay for just four more months, he will receive his diploma. Then he can make other plans. I know he disagrees. He is so weary he can barely think of waiting even four days, let alone four months. I wrote to him to say that all places on the earth are, more or less, the same. It is our state of mind that ultimately determines things. If I were in New York, maybe Steve would find it easier to endure being there. Some day he may even long for the very New York he is so tired of now. It is like my own experience here in this war-torn country. At times, I want to leave it forever. But when I've lived elsewhere, I miss Vietnam so much.

Not long ago, after reading an article about space travel, I imagined myself on a space capsule orbiting the earth. A technical malfunction prevented the rockets on my spacecraft from firing, and I was unable to return to earth. I had no choice but to remain in orbit until my food and oxygen ran out. My radio transmissions to earth were jammed, and I knew I would die utterly alone. No one would know the moment of my death. Even my remains would never return to earth. I felt desperately lonely. I longed for the earth. Cruel and petty people I'd found despicable now seemed as precious as dear friends. I would gladly return to earth, even if I had to spend the rest of my days with them. But there was no way to return, no way to spread my bones on the face of our beloved planet. I could open the capsule's hatch and hurl myself out, but in the absence of gravity I would not fall to earth. The earth no longer wanted me. She no longer pulled me toward herself. I was far removed from earth and humankind.

The constant screaming of jet planes here in Gia Dinh province disturbs the countryside, which would otherwise be quiet and tranquil. The noise makes my head throb. I don't know why they are constantly passing over, but they leave me breathless, like a heavy weight against my lungs. An hour ago I was sitting and playing with a group of children by a haystack. They looked up at the jets with fear, not with the excitement you'd see on children's faces elsewhere. There was no laughter. These children know about the death and destruction that bomb attacks bring on rural villages.

Here you can see and feel the real problems faced by the peasants. Life is simpler here, and it fills my heart with love. I know Steve is not happy living in a society where people spend most of their time pursuing material comfort. I'm not romanticizing poverty, but I have seen people in affluent societies suffer from loneliness, alienation, and boredom, problems unimaginable here.

Several years ago I saw a movie about a woman who was married to a man of some importance. They had a nice home in an elegant neighborhood, two cars, and a large bank account. Their marriage was apparently without friction or turmoil. In the opening scene, the woman was sitting on a chair in their living room, dozing. Her face revealed a vacant weariness bordering on fear, and saliva was dribbling from the corner of her mouth. Suddenly she cried out, and her body shook as though she were struggling with something. Her husband rushed into the room and grabbed her shoulders. She opened her eyes and looked disoriented, but quickly regained her demeanor and smiled cheerfully. The lines of weariness and fear vanished from her face, and she began to chirp gaily like a little bird, "Did you just get home, honey? I must have nodded off. How silly of me. Let me make you a fresh cup of coffee."

Her husband looked at her and asked, "Are you sure you're all right?"

She laughed and said, "Yes, I'm fine. Really, I'm fine."

Then he tells her he has just been summoned to Washington on urgent business and must catch the next plane. He says, "After you've finished making the coffee, can you give me a hand packing?"

She prepares the coffee while he rummages through his closet. The music we have been hearing since the beginning of the film ends. The wife goes to the phonograph and puts on another record. The music is loud with a hard beat. Her husband apparently does not like it, because he comes in, turns it off, and returns to his packing. The woman cannot tolerate silence. She turns the music back on. Irritated, he comes and turns it off again. She turns it on. They go on like this, mindlessly, for several minutes.

After her husband has departed for the airport, the woman sits at home alone. After several albums, she grows weary of listening to music. She picks up a book to read but puts it down after reading only a few lines. She runs to the phone. The first friend she calls is not at home. The second friend she calls is too busy to talk. She can't find anyone to invite over for a cup of coffee and conversation. She hangs up the phone and slumps into a chair, and remains in the same state of *ennui* until late afternoon.

At six o'clock, the newspaper boy knocks at the door. Her face brightens. Perhaps a friend has come. But it is only the newspaper boy. He hands her the paper. She invites him in, but he declines, saying he still has many papers to deliver. Then he looks at her and says, "You ought to check out the corner bar." She feels insulted by his suggestion and quips, "I hardly need that."

After the boy leaves, she feels even lonelier. She thinks about her husband and runs to the phone, dials the operator and says, "I'd like to place a person-to-person call to my husband in Washington, D.C."

The woman hears her husband's voice on the other end of the receiver, and asks, "Did you have a good flight?" "Yes, it was fine," he answers. She cannot think of anything else to say or ask. The phone links two people in distant places. It is almost like having her husband in the same room. But they have nothing to say to each other. Can it be they know everything there is to know about each other after fifteen years of marriage? The woman's mind is blank, so she resorts to asking about the weather. "Is it raining in Washington?"

He answers, "No, the weather is good — clear and warm. I just finished my first meeting." He detects something unusual in his wife's voice and asks, "Are you all right, dear?" It is the second time that day he's asked her that question.

She says, "Yes, I'm fine."

Later, unable to bear the loneliness any longer, she puts on a dress and walks down to the corner bar. It is past midnight and the bar is empty. She orders a shot of whiskey and looks around. A couple enters the bar. The wife goes to the ladies' room and the man sits down near the woman and orders a glass of wine. They share a few words. The woman is clearly lonely and the man obviously finds her attractive. Who knows, perhaps this man, accompanied by his wife, feels lonely, too. They talk some more and laugh. When the wife returns, she makes it clear by her expression that she does not like her husband speaking to another woman. The atmosphere in the bar grows heavy.

Later that night, the woman is plagued by nightmares. In the dim light of her bedroom, we see the same expression of distress and alienation that we saw on her face earlier. She is alone, trapped in a nightmare. Suddenly we hear a key turning in the front door. Her husband has returned from Washington. Entering the bedroom, he sees his wife's distress and rushes to the bed to wake her. She sits up, dazed and confused. Terror is etched on her face. Her husband says, "You didn't sound like yourself on the phone this evening, so I came back as soon as I finished my last meeting. You must be having a nightmare. Are you all right?"

That is the third time he asks the same question. The woman does not answer at once. She can no longer ignore the question, simply saying, "I'm fine." She is not fine. But what is the problem? She doesn't have a physical illness. She doesn't lack material needs. Her home has every comfort, every kind of appliance to make her housework easier. She has a phone in case of emergency. If a burglar breaks in, she can call the police. She is not weak or powerless. She does not need a man's protection from wild beasts or the marauders of an earlier age. Her house is well furnished, she enjoys good health, and her income is more than adequate. Her husband has a good job and is well respected. But everything is not all right. She looks at her husband and admits, "Something is wrong. I'm not fine."

Her problem is common today. People grow lonelier all the time. Take a look at all the religious and social gatherings being organized all the time. Churches and temples have become places for men and women to meet in order to plan get-togethers and parties in the name of religion. Going to church or temple has become a diversion and a way of being seen. People join political committees, women's and men's groups, charitable organizations, student associations, and even groups that oppose nuclear weapons, in order to escape from the emptiness they feel being trapped in the hard shell of themselves. But wherever they go, they continue to spin inside the same shell. Empty social gatherings are just an externalization of that shell.

Steve lives in such a society, and he feels that he can no longer bear it. If he can make contact with the larger world outside his shell of self, even if he remains in the same place, he will not feel so imprisoned. Perhaps he has unconsciously allowed his links to the outside world to become blocked. If he can think about the larger world in which he will swim tomorrow, he will see that his current situation is a necessary step. I hope he will accept his remaining four months at Columbia with a smile. If he can do that, everything will transform before his eyes. The sun will be brighter and the sky more blue. He'll find others friendlier, much easier to get along with.

I think the woman in the film could be healed from her illness if she would just abandon her material comforts for awhile and live instead in a simpler society, perhaps a village in South America or a hamlet like the one I'm now in, someplace where she would have to wash her own clothes in the river. She might cringe when she sees the unsanitary water the villagers drink, but if she lives with the people and shares their concerns, the knowledge she possesses can help the peasants improve their lives. She will undergo hardships and trials, but her smile will begin to radiate like the sun at daybreak. Of course, her liberation will not be without setbacks or challenges. People have a hard time letting go of their suffering. Out of a fear of the unknown, they prefer suffering that is familiar.

The best medicine to chase away the heart's dark isolation is to make direct contact with life's sufferings, to touch and share the anxieties and uncertainties of others. Loneliness comes from locking yourself in a false shell. You think of yourself as a separate, self-contained entity not in relation to others. Buddhists call this "attachment to self." In reality, we are empty of a separate self. But we needn't take the Buddhists' word for it. Looking deeply, we can see that a person is not a separate self.

Literature on alienation is not new. It is easy for people to become fed up and hopeless, feeling that nothing has meaning and that there is no escape. Even the concept "meaningless" feels meaningless. Even the concept "false" feels false. Authors of despair slap another coat of black paint on the whole dismal scene. Even as they claim to be a voice of freedom, their writings contribute to a culture of recklessness and irresponsibility.

Literature promoting the status quo represents one extreme, but literature that advocates complete irresponsibility is another. In the former, at least the writer is still holding on to something. In the second, there is nothing held on to at all. Freedom must not be equated with irresponsibility. Freedom without responsibility is destructive to oneself and others. Literature that promotes freedom without responsibility makes the situation even more desperate. It encourages people to become self-absorbed, hollow, and alienated. Literature of despair claws at our wounds and makes them deeper. We need a literature that guides and heals, and helps us open to the truth about our situation. Understanding our situation is necessary for awareness to emerge. With awareness, we can address the difficulties, make adjustments, and change course. The root causes of alienation can be identified, and when they are identified, they can be healed.

You might laugh at my suggestion to send those who feel alienated to remote, poor villages, but I truly think that if we organized rural hamlets for the lonely, everyone would benefit. These villages would not resemble President Diem's strategic hamlets, but would be more like Princeton or Oxford, places of reflection and retreat. It is hard to heal in a fast-paced city. At Princeton, I heard a student say, "Attending school here is like being in a monastery." But our attitude is what is most important — more important than where we happen to be. Just as it is difficult for germs to overtake a healthy immune system, it is difficult for alienation to overtake inner strength and resolve. The best solution is not to escape from one place in order to go to another, but to develop our solidity, our inner strength.

I am able to write such a long journal entry today, because so many young friends are shouldering the work here. When I was in the United States, I enjoyed the same good fortune. Friends like Steve went to great lengths to help me. I've been thinking about the painful time between June and October 1963. The movement to oppose Diem was gaining momentum in Vietnam, and I had much to do in New York. The phone rang so often my nerves became ragged. I often went without sleep. Thank goodness Steve and other friends were there to lend support. Despite threats and other difficulties we encountered, we never faltered.

I'll never forget the grave expression on Steve's face when he brought me a carton of milk and a chocolate bar to break my fast. I was staying in a meditation room with Japanese tatami mats at the American Buddhist Academy. Steve kneeled down and lovingly poured me a glass of milk. He reminded me of a novice monk. Then he said, "Eat this chocolate bar. It will give you quick energy." It was two in the afternoon, the hour my silent fast was to end. From Monday to Friday afternoon I had meditated on compassion and prayed that freedom would overcome tyranny. I did not eat or drink anything except for the fresh water Steve brought me twice a day.

Immediately after a press conference at Carnegie Hall at which I announced I would fast, Steve scrambled to secure a place where I could meditate undisturbed. I spoke to United Nations Secretary General U Thant about using the meditation hall at the UN, but he hesitated. Finally, he told me that because he himself was Buddhist, he didn't want to appear to be favoring Buddhism. I called the International Church Center at the UN and was told that I could use one of their rooms but that it would cost $300 per day. That meant $1,500 for Monday through Friday! We couldn't afford that kind of money, even if we sold everything we had! I called the American Zen Institute, but they never answered. Finally, the American Buddhist Academy agreed.

The UN General Assembly had begun to discuss the situation in Vietnam. In previous months, I had helped persuade a number of Asian delegates, especially the Ambassador of Thailand, to introduce the subject of Vietnam in the General Assembly's calendar. I gave numerous interviews to newspapers and TV stations. At the Carnegie Hall press conference, organized by an international human rights organization, I said, "The people of Vietnam have already suffered too much. This is the moment we need the entire human family to pray and to act. Immediately after this press conference, I will enter into a silent meditation and fast in order to pray for my homeland. I implore all members of the human family, all who can feel the suffering of Vietnam, to join their prayers for the suffering to stop."

The newspapers printed my call for peace. As Steve

knew, I had reached a point of near-total exhaustion after
trips to Washington, D.C., Chicago, and other cities to
try to raise support for the peace movement back home. I
also assisted with a protest march in front of the White
House, organized by the Association of Overseas Vietnamese. Even young Vietnamese parents carrying infants
joined the march. Many Americans attended, and the TV
networks were all present. It was a moving spectacle.

Unfortunately the meditation room at the American
Buddhist Academy was on the second floor, so I had to
climb a long flight of stairs every time I needed to use the
bathroom. That further drained my strength. Steve did
not allow any reporters or cameramen into the room
during my fast, but when he brought the milk and chocolate, he told me that two TV reporters were waiting to
interview me when I came out of the room.

I held each sip of milk in my mouth and "chewed" it
before swallowing. I ate a piece of the chocolate, although I was skeptical about how energy bolstering it
would be. Steve gave me an update on all that had happened during my fast. He handed me the letters I'd received from Vietnam. There were several birthday cards
— my birthday had passed the day before but I'd completely forgotten it. One card was from my younger
brother. The picture on the card showed an areca grove
half-destroyed by a typhoon. Beneath that image, my
brother wrote, "Rain in the homeland."

Steve spoke to me softly while the TV crews set up

their equipment. He said, "Don't try to speak now. Save your strength for the interview." Luckily the interview lasted only ten or fifteen minutes, unlike newspaper interviews, which can last up to an hour.

Afterward Steve called a taxi, and we went back to our apartment. For the next few days, he took care of everything. He wouldn't let me lift a finger. Steve was a terrible cook, but watching him move around the kitchen warmed my heart. I was used to cooking for him like a mother caring for her son. Now he was caring for me.

It is important to take the time to remember such things, even though life is more than the past. It is also the present and the future. We need to look ahead. Those early days of our rocky and uncertain efforts have passed. Today's problems surround us and we must respond.

Evening has fallen. I will return to the city tonight.

Zen is not merely a system of thought. Zen infuses
our whole being with the most pressing question we
have. It is an urgent life-and-death struggle in which we
either break through or fall into a swirling abyss. It is
necessary for us to face such perilous moments alone,
moments that will determine the rest of our lives. Zen
includes concentrated meditation sessions during which
we might experience one breakthrough after another,
encounter dangers, or die alone in failure. But these
definitions of Zen might only be true for me.

Imagine two young boys coming across an old man
who is sitting in a grassy meadow. The old man tells the
boys that he is fishing for snakes. "This lovely meadow
would be perfect for a flower garden if it weren't for the
poisonous snakes below the ground. I'll fish them out
and stamp them all dead. Then I can prepare my flower
bed," he explains. "There are baby snakes nestled in
snake holes. When I pull them up to the surface, they
wiggle and die. Then there are grown snakes. I have to
be careful when I pull them out, because if I am not
strong enough, they will bite and kill me. You must
know yourself, and you must know the snake. You must

know when you have enough strength and when you don't. When you manage to pull up two snakes at the same time, the best thing to do is to let them fight each other." Fascinated, a little nervous, the boys sit down and watch the old man.

Zen is like that. In the depths of our consciousness dwell the seeds of our potentials, including poisonous snakes, phantoms, and other unsavory creatures. Though hidden, they control our impulses and our actions. If we want freedom, we must invite those phantoms up to our conscious mind, not to fight with them, like the old man fishing for snakes, but to befriend them. If we don't, they will trouble us every day. If we wait for the right moment to invite them up, we'll be ready to meet them, and eventually, they will become benign.

If you were told that you had only two days to live, you might panic, unprepared to deal with such news. Or suppose your beloved tells you that she doesn't love you anymore, that she is in love with someone else. You might be unprepared to cope. You are not prepared for these possibilities, because you have refused to consider them. We do not like to think about things we find frightening or disturbing, so we pretend they don't exist. But if we invite our fears to present themselves and are able to smile at them, things will take care of themselves. But that is not easy to do.

At the beginning of this month, I visited Giac Minh Temple and was alarmed to find Ly sitting in the guest

room handcuffed. Several of Ly's journalist and writer
friends were there, too. Ly's newspaper was closed
down several months earlier, but he has continued to
speak out. When the authorities tried to arrest him, he
went into hiding. He took refuge in Giac Minh Temple,
and his friends tried to persuade him not to leave, fearing for his safety. But he slipped out of the temple, and
within seconds, two men grabbed him. Ly shouted, and
bystanders crowded around to see what was happening.
The men forced Ly to a bus stop where they handcuffed
him to a post, then disappeared. Several people lifted Ly
up so his bound hands could clear the post and he returned to Giac Minh, handcuffed. His friends summoned a locksmith, and they were waiting for him when
I arrived. When he saw me, he laughed, but my throat
was so dry I could not speak. What have we come to?
The authorities grab and handcuff innocent citizens in
broad daylight. My friends and I don't know what will
happen in the coming days, but we are determined not
to hate others, no matter how cruelly they act. We know
that man is not our enemy. Our enemies are ignorance
and hatred.

If I could take Steve on a tour of this village, he
would forget his troubles immediately. This village is
located near some salt marshes, so getting drinking
water during the dry season is difficult. Villagers used to
buy buckets of drinkable water from barges passing by,
and then carry the buckets home on bamboo yokes. But

no one here ever uses the word "buy" or "sell" to describe water, because the Vietnamese word for "water" is the same as the word for "country." No one wants to say he is "selling the country." Country folks hold a deep love for their homeland.

I would take Steve across the dike to show him the new stone-lined tank, six meters deep, that the villagers built with our assistance. The villagers submitted a petition to Public Works, and as a result, Public Works agreed to fill the tank with fresh water three times a week. Now the people can come and fill their buckets whenever they like.

Getting water to drink is only a problem during the dry season. During the rainy season the river fills with fresh water, and villagers can fill their containers with all the water they need. Villagers cultivate large areas of land together and share the harvest equally. Land here does not belong to anyone. It is government-owned land that was abandoned several years ago. Some plants can tolerate the salt water of the marshes, but others can only be planted during the rainy season. A young villager named Bi told us that if you water squash and melon plants with gradually increasing concentrations of salt water, they will become accustomed to it. If Steve were here, I would laugh and ask him if he'd like to be watered with salt water to see whether or not his body would learn to accept it!

Following our suggestions, the villagers started to

grow mushrooms in straw beds to sell. Straw mushrooms bring a good price these days.

The amount of land being cultivated in Vietnam has diminished considerably because of the war. Many villages need to save all their straw for feeding their water buffalo and cattle between harvests, so there aren't as many mushrooms being grown. Other families here are successfully raising New Hampshire chickens purchased by our workers. When we first suggested it, they shook their heads and told us that the chickens they'd tried to raise in the past could not tolerate the salt in the soil where they foraged, and they'd all died. Rather than trying to convince them that it was possible, our volunteers raised a hundred chicks in cages that they built next to the home of a villager named Loi. The cages were warmed by kerosene lamps and filled with sacks of commercially prepared feed. Our workers were careful to maintain sanitary conditions for the chicks and to provide medication whenever needed. In three weeks, the chicks outgrew their cages, and the workers constructed open stalls for them. A constant stream of villagers came to look. Uncle Ba, Aunt Bon, and Grandma Bay were all astonished to see them flourishing. Not one perished. Other villagers came to ask about the project, and as a result, several families decided to raise chickens to supplement their meager incomes.

That is how all the projects evolve in the experimental, self-help villages. First you find out the health care, educational, economic, and social needs of the village. Then you awaken the villagers' interest and support by setting up a demonstration project. One SYSS faculty member, a monk we call Brother Eight, has shown a special talent for winning the hearts of people. We call him a walking encyclopedia, because he is so well-versed in many subjects. It seems there is nothing he does not know. He speaks French, English, and Khmer, in addition to Vietnamese, practices both Western and Chinese medicine, knows how to cultivate oranges, grapefruits, melons, and squash, is a talented teacher, and has the expertise to supervise construction projects. He oversaw the plans and building of the School of Youth for Social Service. When he visits a self-help village, he brings only a small pouch containing areca nuts and leaves, a jar of white elephant balm, some lemons, a bit of cotton, and a few acupuncture needles, and he accomplishes single-handedly what would normally require five or six people. He spoons the backs of the sick and, if necessary, administers first aid or acupuncture, using areca leaves and lemons as medicine. Only rarely does he use pills or injections, yet his patients all improve under his skillful touch; their fevers and pains subside. He is truly gifted. After treating a patient, he sits on a bench and opens up his kerchief to invite the whole family to join him in chewing a mouthful of areca nuts. He talks about the weather and crops. In fact, he can speak about anything and make it interesting. The villagers are quite fond of him. When anyone gets sick, he is the one they summon. Just about everyone feels indebted to him, and in Vietnam even a small debt establishes a strong bond between people. The people enthusiastically support whatever he suggests.

Every village in Vietnam has a small temple with at least one resident monk. If every monk could be convinced to work with us to improve rural life, the movement would succeed in a short time. We don't need war psychology or strategic hamlets. We only need specialists trained in village development, and we are in the process of creating them ourselves. Observing Brother Eight, we understood that basic medicine and acupuncture must be included in the courses at the School of Youth. Our students need to learn how to communicate with the people as effectively and naturally as Brother Eight. If we underestimate the villagers' wealth of experience, we will fail. We need to view the new technologies as supplements to resources that are already there, rather than as replacements for traditional ways. In fact, the School of Youth is more interested in enrolling young men and women from the countryside than from the city, because they understand and can work easily with rural folk.

How the village school got built is an interesting story. One of our workers spent time playing, fishing, and singing with the children. Then he persuaded them to give up a little of their playtime so he could teach them to read and write. They all sat beneath a tree, and he used a flat piece of wood as a blackboard. After only a week, he had a dozen eager students. One village elder who wanted to help them, offered his house as a schoolroom. Then he also donated some wood for benches and other villagers split them into planks. The children were enthusiastic, and their parents were overjoyed to see their children learning to read and write. They knew that in the future others would not be able to look down on their children, and they expressed their gratitude to the teacher. Over time, the number of children increased.

Vietnamese culture was strongly influenced by Chinese culture in the past. According to Confucian traditions, the emperor was the most important person, one's teacher the second, and one's father the third. Emperor, Teacher, Father are "the three filial relations." Confucianism considers a teacher's role important because, like a sage or a saint, he teaches the children virtue. Therefore, if a social worker begins by teaching children, he will win a special place in people's hearts, especially if he teaches the rules of good behavior. Students like to invite their teachers to visit their homes, and they are warmly received there by their parents. This gives an opportunity to discuss the needs of the village in indirect, nonthreatening ways. People are willing to listen to someone they already respect.

When the class in the village elder's home grew too

crowded, parents came together to discuss what to do. Then they initiated action without input from us. They decided to build a village school. Some families donated bamboo, others wood or bricks, and still others their labor. There was no lack of raw materials. A simple building of bamboo, thatch, and earth was enough. When the people see a need clearly, their ability to respond is huge. They are not as poor as we might think, especially in regard to their energy and abilities and the natural resources of the land. Now a school with four classrooms stands, the fruit of the villagers' own efforts. They did not need permission or assistance from the government or any other organization. Two of the school's four teachers are from the village, and the other two will eventually be replaced by villagers, also.

Several young men and women in the village are eager to contribute. Muoi, a fifteen-year-old boy, is one of the most dedicated contributors. It was not always so. His parents both died when he was a child, and he and his nine-year-old half-sister, a lovely child, live with their aunt. Muoi is a fisherman and, although he is young, he shoulders the responsibility of supporting his family. He is more like an adult than a teenager. He used to drink rice liquor every morning before going out on his boat in order to "warm his stomach." In the evenings, he would sit and drink with other men while his sister sold his catch for the day. Every day was the same.

Muoi's aunt is not a warm or kind person, and of

course she couldn't provide Muoi a room of his own, a guitar to play, or books about knights and heroes to read. He had no festivals to attend, no close friends, and no sports to engage in. The only diversions available to him were drinking and gambling. His sister, Muoi Mot, is a student at our Rossignol School. One day she came to school with her eyes red from crying. The teacher asked what was wrong and Muoi Mot said, "My brother left home a week ago and has not returned." The teacher asked where he had gone, and she said that she'd overheard someone say he had found work in an iron foundry in Saigon. When I heard the news I could not help muttering, "Darn! We have lost him to the lure of the city. How could he leave his sister alone with their unsympathetic aunt? I know Muoi loves his sister as much as a mother loves her own child."

A month later, Miss Chin, a School of Youth faculty member who works in the village, saw Muoi in Saigon. At first she did not recognize him in his Western shirt and jeans. The friend he was with had "city" written all over him, but Muoi, on closer inspection, still looked like a country boy. So Miss Chin asked him, "Is it really you, Muoi?"

He was happy to see Miss Chin and answered, "Yes, it is me! Where are you going?" He then turned to his friend and said, "Go on without me. I want to visit with my friend here."

Miss Chin took him to a coffee shop. "I guess you make a lot of money in the city."

"Not at all, Miss. I barely make enough at the iron-works to feed myself. It is no better than being home."

"Then why did you leave the village?"

"Because I felt so bad, Miss Chin. Nothing there is ever going to change. There is nothing happy in my life. I knew that one day I'd be drafted into the army, and that would be the end."

"Don't you care about your sister? You left Muoi Mot on her own."

He didn't answer, but he looked shaken. Miss Chin did not try to persuade him to return to the village. She only asked him where he worked, so that she could visit him from time to time.

"I work at the factory near Dakao, Miss."

Miss Chin offered to pick him up at noon the following Saturday to take him back to the village for a visit. He agreed.

As a result of this experience, teachers in the village and the neighboring villages have begun to organize arts and cultural events. Sometimes the pupils of Love School from Thao Dien Village come over to stage an event, and then the Rossignol pupils reciprocate. Arts and cultural events can be organized at any time. The village elders wholeheartedly pitch in. Many of them contribute by singing traditional folk songs. These events take place on cool, moonlit evenings under the coconut palms, and are enjoyed by all.

The village library is now filled with books, including novels about bold heroes and a complete collection of *The Girl from Do Long*. The sound of the children's happy voices reading Chinese adventure stories to their families at night warms my heart. There is now ping-pong and basketball, too. The teenage "old men" in the village, like Muoi, enjoy these new activities and are giving up their drinking and gambling. Miss Chin threatened them, "I will warn all the young women in these parts not to take any of you as husbands. If they marry you and you go off and get drunk, the whole family will suffer. Only thirteen and fourteen years old, and already drinking!"

At first the young men protested. "We will finds girls from far-off villages then! Anyway, we don't drink that much. Only a little when we're bored." But then they began to see the wisdom in Miss Chin's words, and they told her, "With all the activities now in the village, we can give up drinking easily."

Muoi returned to the village, and his little sister is much happier. He still has to work long hours as a fisherman, but he devotes all his spare time to helping the village. He has become an "elder brother" to many village children, and they love him. He organizes volleyball games and is even learning to play the sitar. He doesn't have the most beautiful voice in the world, but he loves to sing!

I enjoy organizing work like this in the villages, but I have to admit I'm less talented at it than Brother Eight, Miss Chin, and most of the other School of Youth leaders. These wonderful young people have brought about so many successes, it gives me great hope. One could say that I've been the first to benefit from their efforts. The villagers offer me their love, acceptance, and trust, and that renews my dreams. One is always the first beneficiary of one's own good acts. If you sow corn, you reap corn. If you sow beans, you reap beans. Why do we have to go through so many trials before we realize this?

The influence of Phuong Boi is felt here also, even though Phuong Boi is beyond reach in the silent forests of B'su Danglu. The "birds" of Phuong Boi move back and forth between country villages, and Phuong Boi resides in their hearts. Phuong Boi represents love and hope. Someday we hope to be reunited in that cradle of ancient forest.

Will this village and others like it remain safe? Village development moves forward one small step at a time, while war demolishes everything in a few minutes. War does not respect traditions or life. Worst of all, it destroys hope.

On a day as hot as today, returning to the village is as delightful as swimming in a cool river. Breezes blow and the sight of rice fields and palm trees is utterly refreshing. In Saigon, our cramped quarters are unbearably stuffy. The paper ceiling offers no protection from the heat, and by noon we have to go for relief under the areca trees. Such extreme heat takes away our appetites, as well.

A neighbor, Mr. Tu, tried to persuade me to put an air conditioner in the room. He did his best to convince me of the benefits — it would cost some money but it would allow us to accomplish twice as much work. There is truth in that. It is impossible to write when it is this hot. But I decided not to purchase one. Money is not the issue. The rector actually approved the idea and offered to find an inexpensive one. But we would be the only people in our poor neighborhood with an air conditioner, and that would change the way people looked at us. It is one thing to own an old car and quite another to own an air conditioner.

So I looked for another solution. Mr. Bay lives alone in a two-story house next door to the temple. He leaves for work every morning on his motorbike and doesn't return until evening. I asked him if I could use his downstairs room during the day, and he agreed. When I want to write or to work undisturbed by visitors, I just go next door. In Vietnam, friends drop by whenever they feel like it. No one telephones first or makes an appointment. By not being at home, I avoid being rude. I do, however, spend a few hours each day manning the University office, which I must admit is my least favorite activity.

Another solution to the heat is the chilled dessert soup sold by a neighborhood vendor. She makes mung bean and areca flower soups, just like the ones in central Vietnam. I am fond of both kinds. In Vietnamese, sweet soup is called *che*. It is difficult to describe *che* to someone who has never tasted it, but it is delicious. The vendor sells them chilled. Two small bowls on a hot day are as refreshing as a tall glass of cool coconut milk. Unlike me, Hung doesn't like sweets. When I sip *che*, he just watches.

Sometimes the novice Tam, or Brother Man and Brother Toan if they happen by, join me. Toan is now in charge of a publishing house and often drops in at noon. Sometimes he even pays for the bowls of mung bean or areca flower *che* himself. Man is working with Toan. Together, they have a lot of responsibility.

I'll stay in the village this evening to eat supper with Quang and Thu, two of our resident workers. Mrs. Bay brought us two sweet gourds and several cans of sweet rice. The village women look after Quang and Thu as sons or nephews. The gourd soup will be as sweet as the friendship the villagers offer those they trust.

Thu told me about a recent conversation he'd had that touched me deeply. One day, seeing how hard Thu was working, Mr. Bay asked him, "How much money do you make working here?" It is a question we are frequently asked.

Thu answered, "We are not working for money, but for merit, Uncle. Our teacher says that doing good works to help our friends in the village builds merit, the same as doing good works for the temple. The temple provides us with food and a little bus money, but that is the only salary we receive."

Uncle Bay understood, and he looked at Thu with great affection. No doubt he was thinking how fine these young people are. He had thought that city youth were all spoiled and only cared about having a good time. Who would have guessed that there were youngsters concerned about building merit?

Thu's response was perfect, as good as anything to be found in the Buddhist scriptures. His words expressed the meaning of "engaged Buddhism." Merit is an important concept to Asian people. In Sanskrit, merit is called *punya*. In every pagoda in Vietnam, especially in the countryside, laypeople find time to help with whatever work needs to be done. They believe that work done for the pagoda will bear good fruits — material and spiritual — for themselves and their children. The pagoda belongs to all the people; thus anything that benefits the pagoda spiritually benefits the people. Some people donate a few afternoons a month to pagoda service, others three or four days. A few stay at the pagoda for a full month to help out. There are even individuals, generally older, uneducated women, who pledge the rest of their lives to pagoda service. Their practice is expressed through good acts rather than meditation.

Engaged Buddhism in Vietnam teaches that good works do not need to be reserved for the pagoda, but can be extended to towns and villages. Thu explained to Mr. Bay, "People are suffering so much that even the Buddha no longer sits in the temple all the time. The Buddha himself goes out to the people." I was surprised at how skillfully Thu expressed these ideas. Buddha does not just sit in the temple anymore! Of course, the only reason he ever did was because people placed him there. But the Buddha does not want to be isolated amidst offerings of rice, bananas, and flowers. How can a Buddha or a bodhisattva stay indoors? If Bhaisajya Guru (Medicine Buddha) spent all his time in the temple, who would heal the people's wounds of body and spirit? Avalokiteshvara must continue to move if she is to hear and respond to the cries of those who suffer. It does not make sense for students of the Buddha to isolate themselves inside a temple, or they are not his true students. Buddhas are to be found in places of suffering. Thu said it perfectly. We do not need to borrow the words of theologians like Teilhard de Chardin, Karl Barth, or Martin Buber to tell us what to do. We are already, in our own way, bringing about a revolution in Buddhist teaching. Young people like Thu are leading the way into new streams of Buddhist thought and action. They are giving birth to engaged Buddhism.

Religion is one of the few social institutions in Vietnam that remains strong. The political climate and war have dismantled just about everything else. The long siege of troubled affairs has rendered the people suspicious of all official programs and promises. Unfortunately, many politicians want to use religion to serve their own ambitions. Rare is the politician who understands the real potential of religion. Few politicians do anything to support or strengthen religion, because they do not understand the pivotal role religion can play at this moment in Vietnamese history. Most religious leaders don't understand either. That is why I place my faith in the young people. Most leaders, even religious ones, cling to old ways and narrow views. They stand in the way of innovation. It is only because of the unflagging efforts of progressive individuals and their increasingly audible cries of warning that some leaders have finally begun to take notice. Political leaders are like turtles, cautiously poking their heads from their shells to join the race. Our efforts to wake them up must be intensified so that we can transform them from turtles into horses.

Newspaper reports about conflict between Vietnamese Buddhists and Catholics are entirely unfounded. The thoughts and actions of Vietnamese Buddhists and Catholics are, in fact, nearly identical. Put us in a house together to practice our spirituality, and there would be harmony. Spiritual people who see the long view of history recognize the value of reason and dialogue. Though they may follow different traditions, they stand in solidarity. The only conflicts are between those who oppose change and those who courageously strive to bring it about. If we could mobilize the major faiths in Vietnam to join the movement for social progress, we could bring about miracles. The first thing religious bodies could collaborate on would be demanding an end to this catastrophic war.

As I write this, I can visualize the bare wintry trees in Princeton. Vietnam is also passing through a winter of desolation. It is cold and dark, and there is no end in sight. Are our wings strong enough to carry the faith across the long stretches of ice and snow? We do not want to be forgotten by the human family. We are trees stripped of our leaves, enduring ice and snow, day and night. We desperately await the first warm days of spring.

The sky has just unleashed a downpour. No doubt my

room in Saigon is leaking. There are no holes in the tin roof, but rainwater seeps into crevices, then leaks through our paper ceiling. During a storm, we use everything we can to catch the water — wash basins, teacups, pencil holders. The room is probably drenched by now. At this moment, in the midst of this same rainstorm, nearly two hundred School of Youth students are living in self-help villages.

I don't know what tomorrow will bring. But no matter what happens, I don't think my friends will be robbed of their faith. Our faith is not built on shaky ground or esoteric understanding. It is faith in the strength of unconditional love. It asks nothing in return and cannot be shaken even by betrayal. If you take your deepest questions into the core of your being, into your very blood and marrow, one day, quite naturally, you will understand the connection between thought and action. I am not speaking of discursive thought, but of taking your deepest questions into your very soul, of engaging your emotions, your dreams, and all of your experiences, the things most difficult to express in words or concepts. This love arises from the individual psyche, and yet the gradual eroding or sudden destruction of that psyche cannot diminish this love. It is a transcendent, ultimate love. Ordinary love can go up in smoke when confronted by your lover's faults or betrayal. Transcendent love can never diminish, because transcendent love and the objects of that love are both empty of a separate self.

Last year, I went to the British Museum. I was fascinated by the preserved remains of a human body buried
five thousand years ago. The body was lying on its left
side with its knees folded up against its chest. Head,
arms, and legs faced left. Every detail of the man's body
had been preserved. I could see strands of hair, his
ankles, each intact finger and toe. He had been buried in
that position five thousand years ago in the desert. The
heat of the sands had dried and preserved his body. As I
stood engrossed, an indescribable feeling rippled through
my body. A little girl, about eight years old, stood beside
me and asked in a worried voice, "Will that happen to
me?"

I trembled and looked at this tender flower of humanity, this vulnerable child without any means to defend
herself, and I said, "No, this will never happen to you."
Having comforted her, I walked with her into a different
room. I lied about something that Chandaka, the
Buddha's charioteer, never lied about to Siddhartha.

Weeks later, the image of that body returned to me. I
was in Paris meeting with a group of students, and I put
on a tape of Vietnamese songs. As I listened to the voice
of Thai Thanh, I suddenly saw every blood vessel and
every cell of her vocal cords vibrating to produce those
clear and noble sounds. I've never met Thai Thanh, but I
have always pictured her as beautiful and intense as her
voice. I realized that if I could transport myself five
thousand years into the future, Thai Thanh would have

long passed to the other shore. The cassette tape is not
made of living cells, it does not contain saliva or vocal
cords, or the feelings expressed in her lilting voice. Yet
if that tape can still issue the sounds of Thai Thanh's
voice five thousand years from now, what exactly will it
have preserved? A message capable of disturbing the
listener or giving rise to a smile of liberation? A gust of
wind blows across the desert and scatters sand to the
skies. I was reminded of a poem by the Meditation
Master Tran Thai Tong:

> *Storm is gone.*
> *Sky clear.*
> *River reflecting a tranquil moon.*
> *What hour of night is it?*

That night, after walking outside in the snow, I came
down with a cold. Nguyen An spooned my back with
medicated oil, and I took two aspirins before covering
myself with blankets. I was unable to sleep, partly
because of the aspirin. While aspirin alleviates my cold
symptoms, for some reason it always keeps me awake.

I tossed and turned until at one point I realized that I
was lying in the same position as the body in the British
Museum. Without thinking, I pressed my hands together to see if my flesh had hardened into rock. My
conscious mind did not initiate this gesture, but it did
not reject it as silly, either. At that moment I felt per-

fectly at peace. Not one sad or anxious thought entered my mind. I saw that my body as a five-thousand-year-old mummy and my body lying in bed in the present moment are the same. Ideas of past, present, and future dissolved, and I was standing at the luminous threshold of a reality that transcends time, space, and action.

I arose and sat in meditation the rest of the night. Waterfalls of consciousness cascaded through my being. Large raindrops and swirling streams cleansed, penetrated, and fed me. All that remained was a deeply rooted peace. I sat like a mountain and smiled. If anyone had seen me, they might have exclaimed, "He's completed the great task! Tomorrow morning we will see a transformed person." But the next morning, there was no change at all. At seven o'clock, I picked up a pen and jotted down a few impressions of that experience that were hovering at the edges of my consciousness. I still have those notes, odd fragments of poetry. Later I ate breakfast with friends as though nothing had happened during the night. We went over our plans from the previous day's discussion and spoke about the future. Planning for the future? I was back in ordinary time and space.

As I discussed project details, I felt surprised that the same person who felt so removed from such things during the night could now engage in them so easily. From the point of view of my nighttime experience, these projects were transitory flickers in a vast emptiness.

Though I saw that they were more than mere flickers, I
had an entirely different attitude toward them. I could
concentrate wholeheartedly on the details, while my
heart remained completely at ease. I felt no impatience,
fear, or worry, and I had much more energy, as though
the impurities had been filtered from my mind. One
night can change a person's life. One night can open
doors for all other nights. I almost saw my true face; I
was about to break through.

Such an experience helps illuminate the connection
between the world of the mind and the world of action.
What is the place of love? Perhaps nothing I am writing
here will make sense to others. I want to tell Steve not to
worry about a thing. Tomorrow when peace returns to
Vietnam, he will be able to visit Phuong Boi. Phuong
Boi taught us what this love is, and Phuong Boi will
share it with Steve in the language of wildflowers and
grasses. Phuong Boi had a house called Montagnard,
which is now a pile of ashes where wild mushrooms
grow. Yet Montagnard House is still with us. It remains,
just as love remains despite impermanence and emptiness of self, despite so much cruelty and blind ambition.
Tomorrow, if we are burned to ashes, those ashes will be
love and will nestle in the heart of the earth to nourish
the flowers. Flowers don't know how to hate. We will
return to the circle of life as flowers, grasses, birds, or
clouds to bring people the message of eternal love. Like
the village children who, even in this time of war, sing:

"We will love others forever and ever, hand holding hand. We will love others forever."

11 May 1966
Saigon

I t isn't likely that this collection of journal entries, which I'm calling *Fragrant Palm Leaves,* will pass the censors. If it can't be published, I hope my friends will circulate it among themselves. Tonight the sky is strangely bright. I'll leave Vietnam tomorrow, but I already miss home. I know that wherever I go, there will be stars, clouds, and moon, but I am determined to return home. My heart is a little restless, but on the whole I am at peace. I want to share these thoughts, however incomplete, while I'm feeling this calm.

To attain understanding, you have to discard everything you've learned. That is what the *Diamond Sutra* means when it says, "A is only A when it is not A." I know this sounds strange, but the more I live the more I see that it is true. Clinging to what you have learned is worse than not learning it in the first place. Everything I was taught at the Buddhist Institute has been turned upside down. That is why I can understand what I've learned there.

Moments ago, as our DC-4 was approaching Saigon, I saw the most exquisite cloud formations. The sun had already set, but there was enough light in the sky to see the soft, pure clouds spread beneath the airplane like a sea, wave upon curling wave, whiter than the whitest, purest snow. I became one with the clouds, as soft and pure as a cloud. Why are humans so attracted to soft, white clouds and carpets of pure snow? Perhaps it is because we like things that are pure, beautiful, and wholesome, things that reflect the way we want to see ourselves. Purity, beauty, and wholesomeness do not have an objective existence of their own. It is just our viewpoint. We respond to a sheet of white paper, a stream of clear water, a sweet refrain of music, or an attractive man or woman the same way. A beautiful woman is often compared to snow, moon, or flowers. When she is compassionate, we call her a goddess or a Buddha, because goddesses and Buddhas are known to be beautiful and kind. We want to be associated with whatever we consider beautiful, pure, and wholesome, and we want those things to stay the same.

But what about corruption, ugliness, cruelty, and decay? We struggle to remain on the side of the pure and beautiful, and we want to chase the other side away. Mahayana Buddhism describes *nirvana* as permanence, bliss, freedom, and purity. I think the choice of these Four Virtues to describe *nirvana* demonstrates how attached we humans are to a particular idea of happiness.

The *Heart Sutra* was composed to help us shatter such viewpoints. Avalokita, after looking deeply into things, smiles and announces, "All dharmas are marked with emptiness; they are neither produced nor destroyed, neither defiled nor immaculate, neither increasing nor decreasing. Therefore, in emptiness there is neither form, nor feeling, nor perception, nor mental formations, nor consciousness; no eye, or ear, or nose, or tongue, or body, or mind, no form, no sound, no smell, no taste, no touch, no object of mind."

As I sat on the plane, I saw all this from a different perspective. I smiled as I thought about the different forms water takes. It can be a clear liquid, ice, steam, clouds, or snow. All these forms are H_2O, but H_2O itself is empty, without permanence. It can be broken down into hydrogen and oxygen, but they, too, are empty. Examine oxygen and you will see that it is made up of non-oxygen elements, which are also empty and made of other elements. They are all interdependent and inter-connected. You cannot separate oxygen from non-oxygen, but neither can you say that oxygen and non-oxygen are the same.

In this world of constant change, we want to hold on to some permanent, ultimate truth. Suppose I ask myself what is the most beautiful and important thing in the world, and suppose I answer "water." Water can be clear as a mirror. It can cover a mountain peak or become swirling white waves by the seashore. Without water, the earth would dry up and perish. Therefore, I say that water is the most beautiful and important thing. But if I pause and consider fire, I realize that life could not be

possible without the light and warmth of the sun either.
In fact, without light, how could anyone distinguish
what is beautiful from what is not? Without light, who
could see water clear as a mirror, snow covering a mountain peak, or waves swirling by the seashore? I might
grasp this truth, but if I am obsessed with water, I will
close my eyes and cling to water alone. That would be
ignorance, wouldn't it?

Some argue that the continual transformation of phenomena supports a belief in reincarnation. You may have
discarded that belief when you were still young, understanding that it presumes the existence of some separate,
permanent self or soul that can transmigrate. In reality,
there is no separate self, no oxygen or hydrogen with a
separate, permanent identity. Yet the world of emptiness
reveals itself as eternally miraculous. There is a kind of
reincarnation, although if we look deeply, we will see
that nothing is permanent or impermanent, pure or
corrupt, kind or cruel, beautiful or ugly. Please do not
repeat these things to children because their eyes are not
open wide enough yet. They may conclude that there is
no reason to live in accord with ethics if there is neither
good nor evil.

Given a choice, wouldn't you choose purity over
corruption, happiness over suffering, kindness over
cruelty? That seems obvious. But to choose purity,
happiness, and kindness, most people assume that we
have to destroy corruption, suffering, and cruelty. Is it

possible to destroy them? If the Buddha's teaching,
"This is, because that is," is true, then within purity
there is corruption. If you destroy corruption, you si-
multaneously destroy purity. "This is not, because that is
not." Does that mean we should nurture corruption,
cruelty, and suffering? Of course not!

All pairs of opposites are created by our own minds
from our store consciousness. We make happiness and
suffering into an enormous struggle. If we could only
penetrate the true face of reality, as Avalokita did, all
our sorrows and misfortunes would vanish like smoke,
and we would indeed "overcome ill-being."

Look at the Buddha's smile. It is completely peaceful
and compassionate. Does that mean that the Buddha
does not take your and my suffering seriously? The
Buddha sent Bodhisattva Sadaparibhuta to inform us
that the Buddha does not look down at anyone, because
every being will become a Buddha.

Maybe my response to the Buddha's smile is caused
by a childish sense of inferiority — it certainly does not
arise from a feeling of self-respect. It is easy for us to feel
insignificant, clumsy, and stupid before the Buddha,
who sees *nirvana* and *samsara* as mere flickers of emptiness. Yet I am certain that the Buddha feels compassion
for us, not because we suffer but because we do not see
the path, and that is the cause of our suffering.

Since I was a young man, I've tried to understand the
nature of compassion. But what little compassion I've

learned has come not from intellectual investigation but from my actual experience of suffering. I am not proud of my suffering any more than a person who mistakes a rope for a snake is proud of his fright. My suffering has been a mere rope, a mere drop of emptiness so insignificant that it should dissolve like mist at dawn. But it has not dissolved, and I am almost unable to bear it. Doesn't the Buddha see my suffering? How can he smile? Love seeks a manifestation — romantic love, motherly love, patriotic love, love for humanity, love for all beings. When you love someone, you feel anxious for him or her and want them to be safe and nearby. You cannot simply put your loved ones out of your thoughts. When the Buddha witnesses the endless suffering of living beings, he must feel deep concern. How can he just sit there and smile? But think about it. It is we who sculpt him sitting and smiling, and we do it for a reason. When you stay up all night worrying about your loved one, you are so attached to the phenomenal world that you may not be able to see the true face of reality. A physician who accurately understands her patient's condition does not sit and obsess over a thousand different explanations or anxieties as the patient's family might. The doctor knows that the patient will recover, and so she may smile even while the patient is still sick. Her smile is not unkind; it is simply the smile of one who grasps the situation and does not engage in unnecessary worry. How can I put

into words the true nature of Great Compassion,
mahakaruna?

When we begin to see that black mud and white snow
are neither ugly nor beautiful, when we can see them
without discrimination or duality, then we begin to grasp
Great Compassion. In the eyes of Great Compassion,
there is neither left nor right, friend nor enemy, close nor
far. Don't think that Great Compassion is lifeless. The
energy of Great Compassion is radiant and wondrous.
In the eyes of Great Compassion, there is no separation
between subject and object, no separate self. Nothing
that can disturb Great Compassion.

If a cruel and violent person disembowels you, you
can smile and look at him with love. It is his upbringing,
his situation, and his ignorance that cause him to act so
mindlessly. Look at him — the one who is bent on your
destruction and heaps injustice upon you — with eyes of
love and compassion. Let compassion pour from your
eyes and don't let a ripple of blame or anger rise up in
your heart. He commits senseless crimes against you and
makes you suffer because he cannot see the way to
peace, joy, or understanding.

If some day you receive news that I have died because
of someone's cruel actions, know that I died with my
heart at peace. Know that in my last moments I did not
succumb to anger. We must never hate another being. If
you can give rise to this awareness, you will be able to

smile. Remembering me, you will continue on your path. You will have a refuge that no one can take from you. No one will be able to disturb your faith, because that faith does not rely on anything in the phenomenal world. Faith and love are one and can only emerge when you penetrate deeply the empty nature of the phenomenal world, when you can see that you are in everything and everything is in you.

Long ago I read a story about a monk who felt no anger toward the cruel king who had chopped off the monk's ear and pierced his skin with a knife. When I read that, I thought the monk must be some kind of god. That was because I did not yet know the nature of Great Compassion. The monk had no anger to hold back. All he had was a heart of love. There is nothing to prevent us from being like that monk. Love teaches that we can all live like the Buddha.

Tomorrow morning I must depart. I won't have time tonight to read over what I have written, but I will see Hung briefly tomorrow and I'll give him this manuscript before I leave our blessed homeland.

Plum Village is a retreat community in southwestern France, where monks, nuns, laymen, and laywomen practice the art of mindful living under the guidance of Thich Nhat Hanh. Visitors are invited to join the practice for at least one week. For information, please write to:

Plum Village
13 Martineau
33580 Dieulivol, France
www.plumvillage.org

Parallax Press publishes books and tapes on Buddhism and related subjects to make them accessible and alive for contemporary readers. It is our hope that doing so will help alleviate suffering and create a more peaceful world. We carry all books and tapes by Thich Nhat Hanh. For a copy of our free catalog, please write to:

Parallax Press
P.O. Box 7355
Berkeley, California 94707
www.parallax.org